David Tajchman   Project Process Progress

Gran Mediterraneo

Contents

Forewords

7 Too Beautiful
11 Future Collectivism

Project

17 The White City, Curves and Concrete
33 High-Rises and Contemporary Architecture in the White City
49 Kibbutz Collectivism
59 Public Shared Vehicles
75 Carchitecture
83 Radiant Cities

Process

97 Vertical (Car) Park
105 Loci Plasticity
117 Circular Landscape Urbanism
133 Endlessness
145 Form Finding

Progress

159 Digital Translation
175 Vertical Kibbutz
177 Drawings
184 Programme
201 Appendix
206 Acknowledgements

Too Beautiful

> "The past does not exist.
> Everything is simultaneous.
> In our culture only the present
> exists in our idea of the past
> and our vision of the future."
> — Gio Ponti

We live in a period of reaction.
The problems of a mutating world bring
the challenges of global change to
the forefront of public debate.
And change is clearly frightening. Images
of "corporate" investment compete with
a return to modest means, a return to
"history", to "identity", to an architecture
of "simplicity" and "authenticity".
Our faith in the future seems shaken.

But architecture is an optimistic endeavour.
It is about projecting buildings that
are not there yet. It is, by definition, about
inventing a future. Giving form to a vision
of the best in our contemporary world,
even a social vision, therefore implies
visionary architecture. In our post-utopian
era, architecture can still invent
progressive forms.

Gran Mediterraneo seeks to embody social progress. It melds cultural innovation and technical evolution with architectural invention. It is, in sum, a prospective project with clear ambitions for our present.

This is no flight of futuristic fancy: all ingredients are clearly part of a common heritage and a dynamic contemporary environment, waiting to be fused into a new entity. It is a form of prescience that lies in reading the signs of the present.

Finding new solutions for our society is an opportunity to find new forms of interaction, and spaces enabling new uses. Sited in an iconic site, in a comfortable neighbourhood, the Gran Mediterraneo asserts itself by fusing familiar local references - curving white concrete, the tower, the car - into an endless loop of activity.

A superficial look at the project may deceive, for this is not luxury housing or some flamboyant hotel. Here is a hive of communal activity: co-housing, co-working, co-driving. With an affirmed presence on a central plaza, it gives clear priority to shared civic space.

The spiralling interiors of the tower explore generative links in the hybrid program. They suggest a possible form for new relationships in a shared economy, where virtual and physical exchanges can happen, perhaps on new terms. At a close reading, the diverse plans and sections show potential for a literally fluid environment, and also reveal the challenges that such openness entails, challenges that are taken here as an opportunity to find alternative solutions. These solutions would embody the intuitive space of virtual networks, rather than the industrial logic of orthogonal space.

The hybridization leads to sensual curves, a generous image of the potential of the different programs. An image of intertwined destinies remarkably appropriate for the melting pot that the geographic context provides. A positive image, particularly in troubled times.

Too beautiful?

Gran Mediterraneo is as ambitious
a project as one could hope for.
It seeks to embody the best elements
of a current context. As such it
is an aspiration for the Eastern
Mediterranean, the Middle East,
the crossroads of Occidental and
Oriental cultures. Beyond aesthetics,
it is a beautiful vision.

— Carl Fredrik Svenstedt

Future Collectivism

Integrating vertical farming and public autonomous vehicles in a collective living in the Mediterranean area.

Gran Mediterraneo, a Tel Aviv-specific mixed-use high-rise, is about integrating the characteristics of living in a Mediterranean environment into a hybrid and three-dimensional program that is subject to an urban horizontal sprawl. Beyond the idea of building tall or super-tall, which is not the initial purpose of this project, but more of vertically breaking with the traditional stacking of horizontal slabs and, more critically, with the ongoing developments of the Tel Avivian skyline, the Gran Mediterraneo experiments the vertical setting of a topological geometry that welcomes local nature and technologies, resulting into a tower that is spiralling, endless and flourishing.

Using the social typology of the Kibbutz (and the Moshav) as a vehicle for investigation, the tower takes inspiration in the Israeli version of agricultural co-housing.

Parallel to this investigation is
a study of collective living integrated
with urban agriculture: a vertical
city discussing when the separation
between architecture and agriculture
blurs away and everything blends
into a single entity.

The Gran Mediterraneo tower is
situated in the White City,
a UNESCO World Cultural Heritage
designated site in Tel Aviv, where
low-rise constructions from the 1930s
belong to the International Style,
Art-Deco and Bauhaus movements.
The citation recognized the unique
adaptation of modern international
architectural trends to the cultural,
climatic, and local traditions of
the city. Inspired by the curves of
the concrete painted white, which
is predominant in the city, and
paying tribute to this plasticity,
Gran Mediterraneo innovates with
its specific topological geometry to
be built with white dyed concrete.
The curvy concrete extends to its
immediate surrounding public space,
integrating its circular geometry into
a ground parametrical arabesque
based on a circle proliferation.
Aiming to become a vertical

architectural landmark in the Tel Avivian skyline and perhaps in the Middle-Eastern Mediterranean area, it searches for a specific architectural identity that evokes a cultural mix of Orient and Occident.

The case-study site, located in a Mediterranean city, is the biggest pedestrian public space in the city. Kikar Hamedina is symbolic, circular and was designed by Brazilian architect Oscar Niemeyer in the 1970s. Surrounded by a repetitive brutalist building, the circular plaza is nowadays being gentrified, becoming a hub for luxury boutiques. Located midway between the freeway and the beach, in a residential area, this proposal is an opportunity to eco-design components of urban farming and develop related applications through investigation into the social characteristics of a kibbutz. It offers another view on how we can apply the collective ideal into an urban environment congested with car traffic and gated community high-rises.

This collective scheme is enriched by a shared car system for the city. Driverless, public, and electrical vehicles represent a futuristic symbol of freedom and social equity. The tower features a car-silo equipped with robotic car-parking, emerging from the plaza's underground. The vertical car-park is a response to the current lack of parking lots in the city and the inadaptation of the city to its rising number of vehicles. The tower acts as the first metropolitan station for regular and driverless vehicles as well as an electrical station for vehicles to charge batteries by induction.

Mediterranean nature, white concrete and autonomous shared vehicles are the three components of this self-initiated high-rise, merging ecological needs with local and technological inventions both in the process of building as well as during the building's life and usage. Co-housing, co-working, co-moving, and vertical farming make the collective spirit of the Gran Mediterraneo, translated into programmatic landscapes all along the tower's height.

— David Tajchman

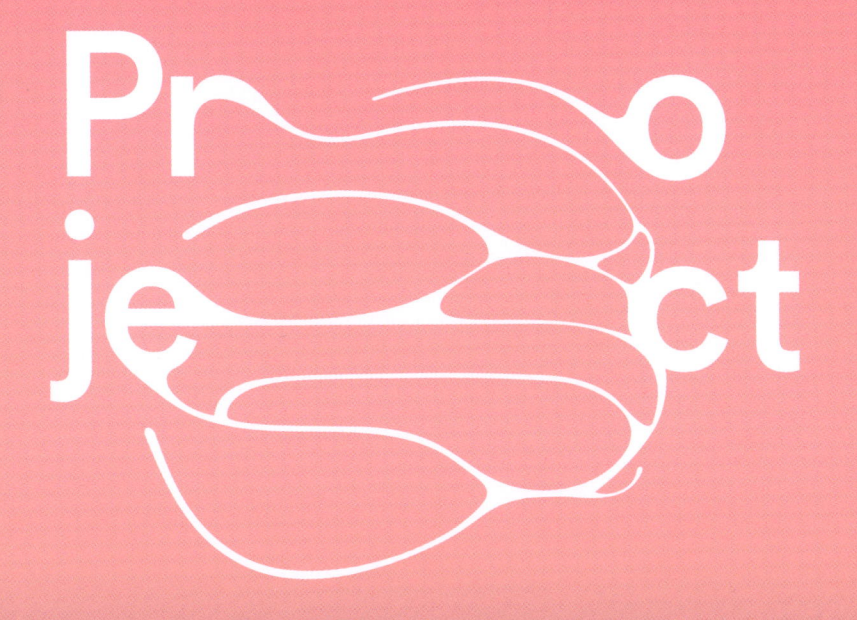

Project

The White City, Curves and Concrete

Tel Aviv-Jaffa is a city situated along the Mediterranean coastline in Israel. The modern city of Tel Aviv was founded in 1909 at the time of the Ottoman period, in the neighbourhoods of Jaffa, a harbour city. Tel Aviv and Jaffa were merged in 1950. The city, also called "the city that never sleeps" due to its young population and its dynamism, or "the bubble" for its peaceful and respectful atmosphere, is quite detached from the conflicts in the region.

Tel Aviv's White City, designated a UNESCO World Heritage Site in 2003, comprises the world's largest concentration of International Style buildings (Bauhaus, Art Deco, and other related modernist architectural styles).

White concrete low-rise buildings with their rounded edges and their long curvy balconies constitute the landmarks of Tel Aviv's architectural identity. The Gran Mediterraneo pays tribute to the curvy white concrete of the city, avoiding pastiche of the existing legacy.

18 Tel Aviv-White City 1930s

01 Photomontage
Moshe Vrobitzky
1934

1930s

Tel Aviv-White City

02

02 Aerial photograph of Northern Tel Aviv
    and Dizengoff Circle

03 Braun House
    49 Ahad Ha'am Street / Mazeh Street
    Zaky Chelouche Architect

04 Soskin House
    12 Lilienblum Street
    Ze'ev Rechter Architect

Tel Aviv-White City

1933

03

04

1934

Tel Aviv-White City

05

05 The Ship House (Shimon Levi House)
56 Lavandah Street / Hamasger Street
Arieh Cohen Architect

06 31 Mazeh Street
M. Rosengarten Architect

22 Tel Aviv-White City 1934

06

1934

Tel Aviv-White City

07

08

Tel Aviv-White City

1935

09

07 Feldmann House
18 Bialik Street
Emanuel & Eliyahu Friedman Architects

08 Biegelmann House
11 Shlomo Hamelekh Street / Tel Hai Street
Avraham Kabiri Architect

09 Reisfeld House
96 Hayarkon Street
Pinchas Biezunsky Architect

1935

Tel Aviv-White City

10 Shalem House
    28 Rosh Pina Street
    Arieh Cohen Architect

11 Buxenboim House
    6 Bilu Street
    Arieh Streimer Architect

12 Bruno House
    3 Strauss Street
    Ze'ev Haller Architect

Tel Aviv - White City

1935

12

27 1935   Tel Aviv - White City

13

1935

14

13 Leon Recanati House
35 Menahem Begin road /
79 Mazeh Street
Salomon Liaskowsky &
Jacov Ornstein Architects

14 Shaltiel House
3 Nachalat Binyamin Street
Arieh Cohen Architect

15 Greenberg House
39 Trumpeldor Street
Shlomo Erlich Architect

15

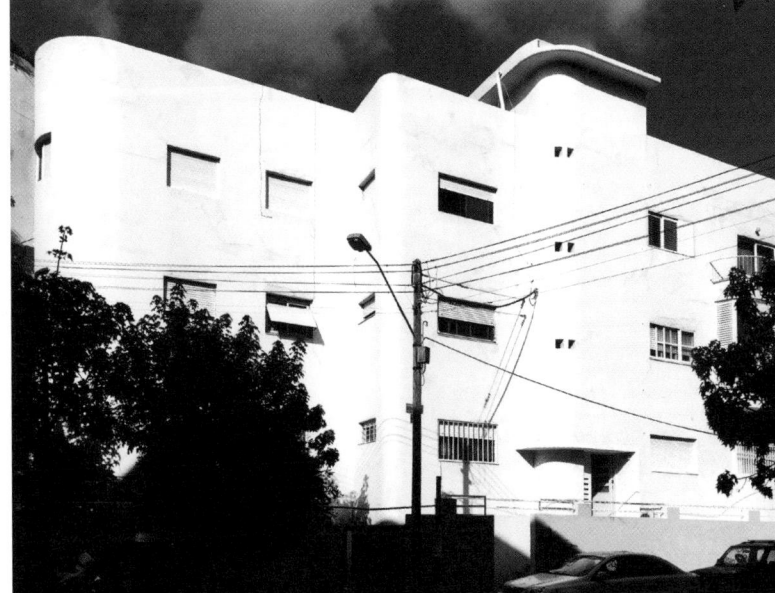

1936

Tel Aviv-White City

16 House Ben-David
60 Frishman Street
Aaron Shiffman Architect

17 Hornstein House
48 Dizengoff Street / 54 King George Street
Ze'ev Haller Architect

Tel Aviv-White City

1936

17

1937

Tel Aviv-White City

18

18 Ya'acov Hanoch House
   10 Aharonovitch Street / Glickson Street
   Richard Barzilai & Shmuel Haussmann Architects

19 Esther Cinema (formerly Dizengoff Cinema)
   Zina Dizengoff Circle / 1 Zamenhof Street
   Yehuda & Raphael Magidovitch Architects

32 Tel Aviv-White City 1939

19

High-Rises and Contemporary Architecture in the White City

As other cities across the world, Tel Aviv started to see rising on its skyline several skyscrapers in the 1960s, but with very few of them bearing in mind its 1930s much acclaimed legacy. This trend that started in the 1960s, with the fast-growing socio-economic development of the country, continues to the present. Today, Tel Aviv architectural landscape shows several contemporary high-rises exhibiting neither Mediterranean specific characteristics, nor any relation to its 1930s heritage. They seem to project on the skyline an image out of context, as if they could have been designed anywhere else, but Tel Aviv. While socio-economic development is important for the life of the city, a more progressive architectural vision would transform the material matter in terms of heritage, nature, and local culture, to preserve the inner soul of the White City.

The current high-rises projects usually offer high standards of luxury with various amenities such as gym, lounge, rooftops, safety fences, guards, and other urban modern comforts. They are conceived almost as gated vertical communities, golden cages, expensive to afford, comparable in price to skyscrapers found in many other international megacities. Often, the interior decoration, rather than the overall architectural design, takes the front line in the project development.

Since the early 2000s, artists, designers and architects have produced artworks or design works paying tribute to the White City, bringing back Tel Aviv to the forefront of the Avant-Garde in the Mediterranean area. There is a potential to conceive tall buildings in the White City, while bearing in mind local history, tradition, knowledge, culture, nature, architecture, economy, and lifestyle. Gran Mediterraneo seeks to be a White City-specific high-rise.

High-Rises Timeline

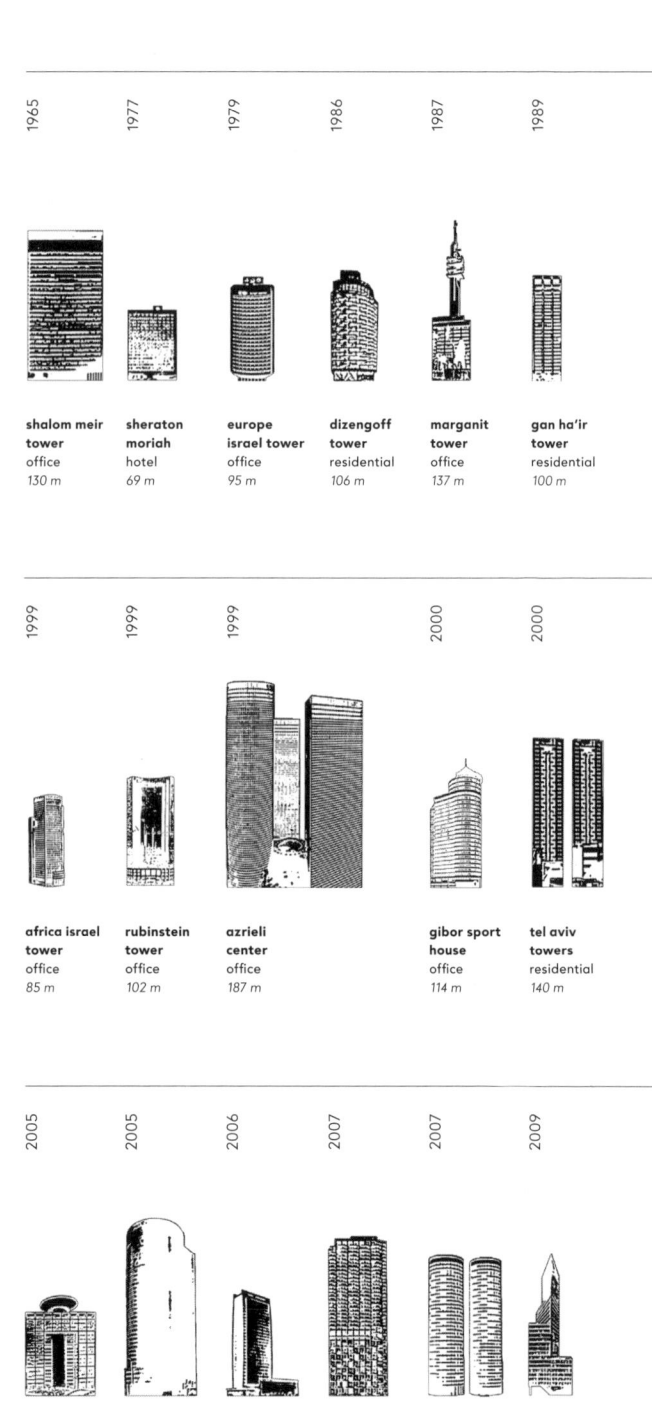

1965	1977	1979	1986	1987	1989
shalom meir tower office 130 m	**sheraton moriah** hotel 69 m	**europe israel tower** office 95 m	**dizengoff tower** residential 106 m	**marganit tower** office 137 m	**gan ha'ir tower** residential 100 m

1999	1999	1999	2000	2000
africa israel tower office 85 m	**rubinstein tower** office 102 m	**azrieli center** office 187 m	**gibor sport house** office 114 m	**tel aviv towers** residential 140 m

2005	2005	2006	2007	2007	2009
matcal tower office 107 m	**hayovel tower** office 158 m	**bank discount tower** office 105 m	**neve tzedek tower** residential 147 m	**yoo towers** residential 128 m	**first international bank** office 132 m

High-Rises Timeline

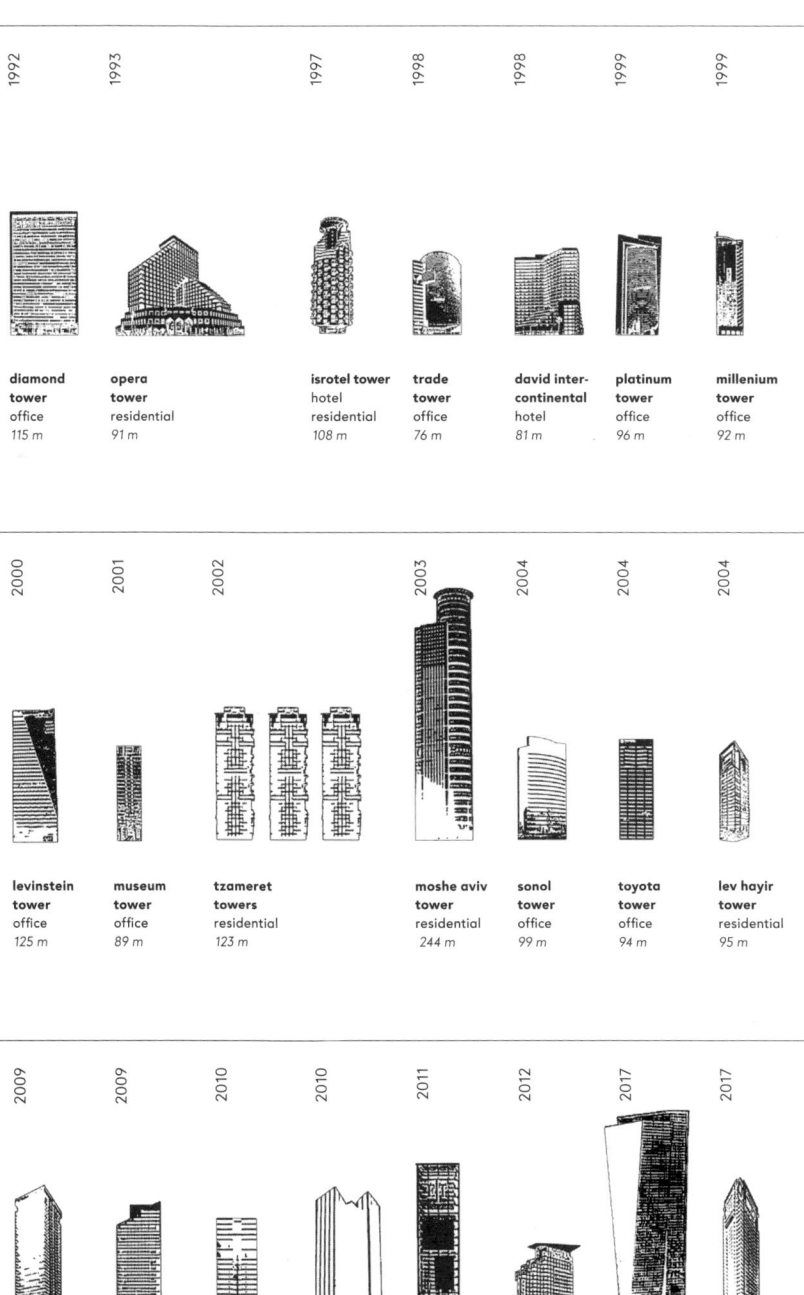

37 1963 High-Rises

20

High-Rises

1964

21

20 EL AL Building
    Dov & Ram Karmi & Zvi Meltzer Architects

21 Metzudat Zeev (Beit Jabotinsky)
    Mordecai Ben Horin Architect

39 | 1965 | High-Rises

22

22　Shalom Meir Tower
　　Yitzhak Pearlstein, Gideon Ziv
　　& Meir Levy Architects

23　Spiral High-Rise
　　Zvi Hecker with Alfred Neumann
　　& Eldar Sharon Architects

High-Rises

1965

23

1976

White City Legacy

24

24 Asia House
    Mordecai Ben Horin Architect

25 Dizengoff Residential Tower
    Mordecai Ben Horin Architect

High-Rises

1985

1989

Spiral High-Rise

26

26 Spiral Apartment House
Zvi Hecker Architect

27 Azrieli Center
Eli Attia + Moore Yaski Sivan Architects

High-Rises

2007

27

45

2011

White City Legacy

28

28 Tel Aviv Museum of Art
    Preston Scott-Cohen Architects

29 Tel Aviv Museum of Art
    Preston Scott-Cohen Architects

White City Legacy

2011

29

High-Rises Artwork

2011

2017

31

30 "Deportation"
   Détournement of the Azrieli Center
   Victor Enrich Visual Artist

31 Rothschild Tower
   Richard Meier & Partners Architects LLP

Kibbutz Collectivism

Envisioning a vertical city in the Mediterranean area, while breaking with the usual stacking of identical horizontal slabs, Gran Mediterraneo proposes a new programme and activities for shared civic spaces, and a better mix of comforts that we habitually find in a horizontal city.

Kibbutzim and Moshavim are agricultural (social) communities that appeared in Israel in 1909. They were then progressively multiplied in the whole country until the 1980s, when several of them started to get privatized. With its collective spirit, the Kibbutz shows the possible foundation of a city by and for all generations and all education levels and backgrounds. Integrating all activities that are shared by the inhabitants, it shows different planning layouts whether located on a hilly or a flat ground. It is an experimental way of conceiving a new village or a city, where the agricultural starting point resonates with nowadays ideas of integrating farming into a contemporary vertical architecture. The Gran Mediterraneo develops its own proposed Kibbutz-inspired programme of mixed use activities in a vertical setting.

Kibbutz Timeline

1909
degania
kibbutz
umm juni

1921
gan schmuel
kibbutz
hadera

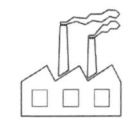

1921
nahalal
kibbutz
rehovot

1928
givat brenner
kibbutz
rehovot

1932
ma'abarot
kibbutz
sharon plain

1944
shamir
kibbutz
upper galilee

1946
ein tzurim
kibbutz
gush etzion

1949
megiddo
kibbutz
jezreel valley

1980
privatization of kibbutzim

1921

Radiant Collectivism

32 Aerial view of Moshav Nahalal
from southeast to northwest
Richard Kauffmann Architect

33 Workers in the field, training period of the new
immigrants at Kibbutz Na'an

Kibbutz Farming

1935

33

53 1935 — Kibbutz Farming

34

34 Members of the Mahanot Haolim loading hay at Kibbutz Na'an

35 A student taking care of chickens at Moshav Nahalal

36 Ziva Heifetz (on the right) and her friend Ella at Moshav Nahalal

37 Potted plants in the nursery at Moshav Nahalal

Kibbutz Farming

1940s

35

36

37

1940s

Kibbutz Upbringing

56 Kibbutz Celebrations

1940s

41

42

38 First girls born in Kibbutz Bet Hashitta

39 Children near an artificial lake
    at Kibbutz Merhavya

40 Children at Kibbutz En Harod

41 Girls celebrating the first fruits
    at Kibbutz Merhavya

42 Seder Pesach at Kibbutz Merhavya

57

1940s

Kibbutz Activities

43

44

45

Kibbutz Arts

1940s

46

47

43 Summer camp children valley

44 Volleyball players

45 The first camp headquarters of the kibbutz members at Kibbutz Giv'at Brener

46 Music class in Ramat Hadassah Szold

47 Painter working at Kibbutz Merhavya

Public Shared Vehicles

Tel Aviv suffers from lack of an appropriate public transportation network, permanent traffic jams and lack of parking spaces. The White City is not well-prepared to accommodate the growing number of cars and Tel Avivians are hooked on wild parking on the sidewalks of their city. Works have started for the construction of a subway in the metropolitan area to be completed by 2024. Alternatively, an old efficient solution exists in the country: the Sherut, a collective taxi van that replaces the absence of efficient public transportation systems. Fluid and fast, Sherutim drive in and in-between cities in Israel.

Inspired by the Autolib' (shared electric car system) in Paris, and earlier futuristic visions of driverless cars, the Gran Mediterraneo includes an automated car-silo for shared autonomous vans and regular vehicles. This public charging station would be the first in Tel Aviv and the world. The Future Sherut is designed driverless and charging by induction when parked in its station

60 in the Gran Mediterraneo. This autonomous vehicle and the high-rise's vertical car-park have been designed together as a holistic and futuristic vision for an autonomous transportation network for the White City.

48

48 Shared electric vehicle
    Golf cart at Kibbutz Sha'ar Ha'Amakim
    2016

2017

Sherut

49 Collective Intercity Taxi, Israel

50 Ayalon highway, Tel Aviv

62 Everyday Traffic 2017

50

2024

Tel Aviv Metropolitan Area Mass-Transit System

51 Works on Menahem Begin Boulevard

Driverless Electric Vehicles Timeline

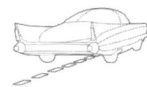

1956
'electricity may be the driver'
electric induction charging while driving
central power & light company, usa

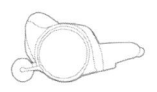

1958
self driving vehicles
broadacre city
frank lloyd wright, usa

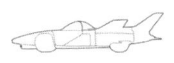

1960
self driving car
electronically controlled firebird
general motors, usa

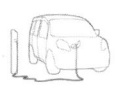

2008
battery switching services
better place
renault, israel

2010
self driving van
personal rapid transit
masdar city

2011
shared electric car
autolib'
paris, france

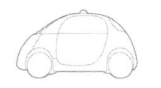

2014
self driving car
google, usa

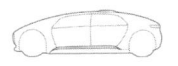

2015
self driving car
mercedes-benz, germany

1933

Hybrid Concept Car

52

52 Buckminster "Bucky" Fuller - Fly's Eye Dome and Dymaxion Car

53 Citroën constantly innovating for comfortable driving

Technology Pioneer

1955

1956

Autonomous Vehicles

54

ELECTRICITY MAY BE THE DRIVER. One day your car may speed along an electric super-highway, its speed and steering automatically controlled by electronic devices embedded in the road. Travel will be more enjoyable. Highways will be made safe—by electricity! No traffic jams ... no collisions ... no driver fatigue.

Autonomous Vehicles

1960

55

54 Electricity May Be The Driver

55 Firebird III, General Motors, Motorama

2008–11

Shared Public Vehicles

56

57

56 Charging stations, Better Place,
    Electric battery switching station, Israel

57 Autolib', electric, Cecomp, Pininfarina Design, Paris

58 Driverless Personal Rapid Transit (PRT) system,
    electric, Masdar City

59 Waymo self-driving vehicle
    California, USA

Autonomous Vehicles

2010–14

58

59

2015

Autonomous Vehicles

60

Mercedes-Benz F015

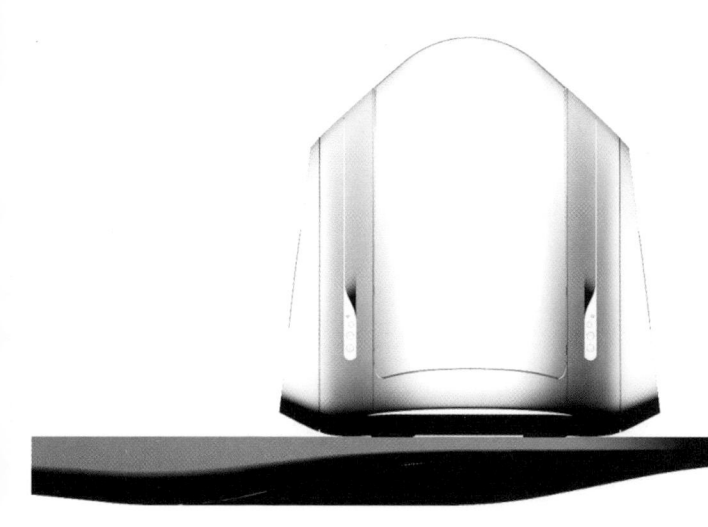

Future Sherut

2016

Gran Mediterraneo's Telavivian collective autonomous vehicle, front view
David Tajchman Design

2016

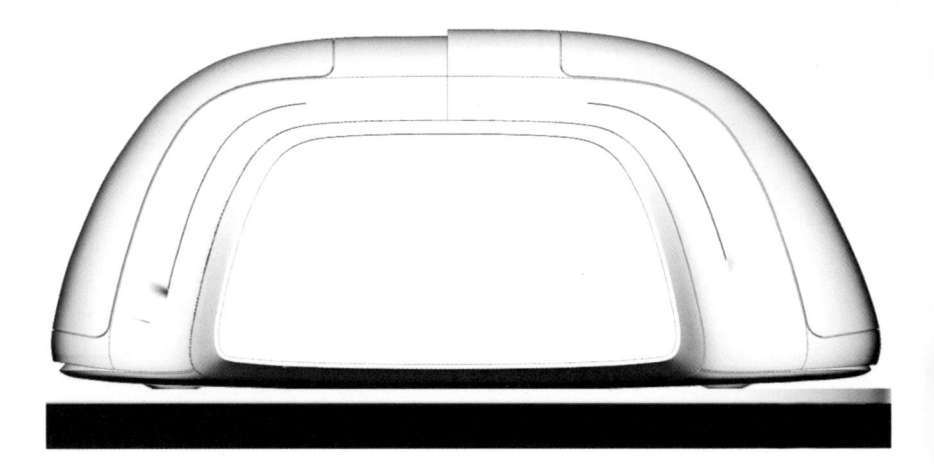

Future Sherut

Gran Mediterraneo's Telavivian collective autonomous vehicle, side view
David Tajchman Design

74   Future Sherut   2016

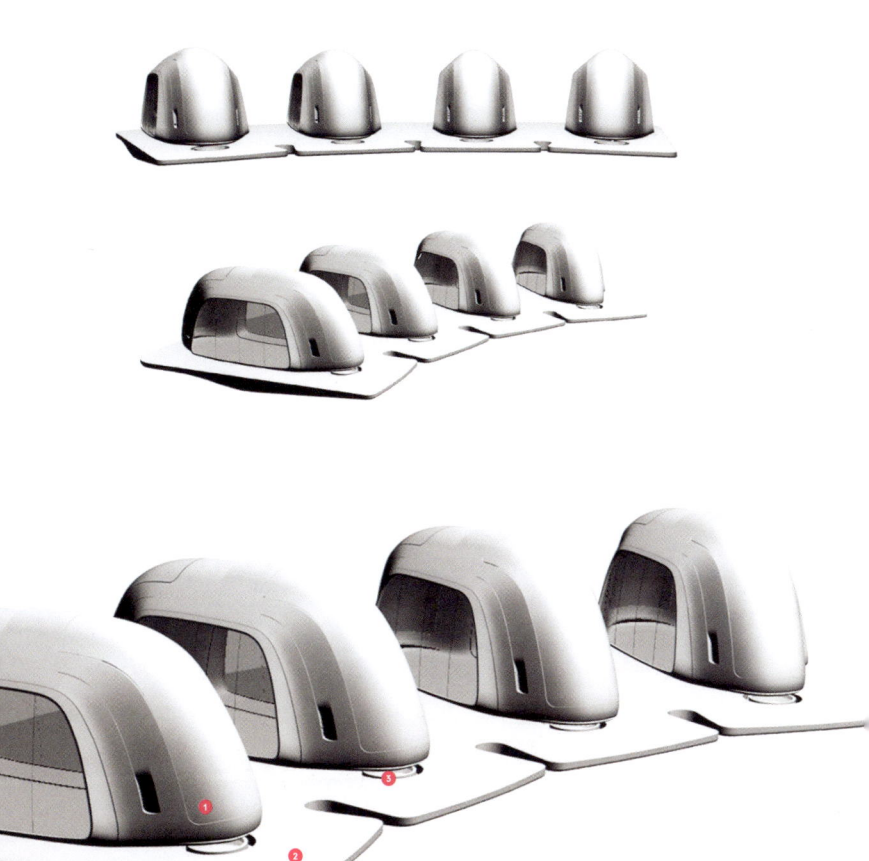

❶ future sherut
❷ gran mediterraneo silo's radial concrete parking spaces
❸ induction charging and lighting device

Gran Mediterraneo's Telavivian collective autonomous vehicle, induction charging station
David Tajchman Design

Carchitecture

Throughout recent history, Architecture and Car Manufacturing show a special relation: an evolution related to progress in vehicle design and the way to park it. Ramps and obliques are progressively replaced by robots and by automated parking, turning the initial infrastructure into silos and vertical car-parks.

Considering the vehicle as an integral part of the city and as a symbol of freedom throughout history since the early 1900s, the Gran Mediterraneo pursues the idea of integrating the car as a prominent part of the programme. The high-rise's layout and dimensions first sketches started with the car's needs in terms of space, gyration and necessary technology to manoeuvre on automated platforms.

Gran Mediterraneo places the vehicle at the heart of the proposal and as a design starting point, aiming to find an appropriate solution for Tel Aviv and its congestion problems. A spiralling Mediterranean nature park surrounds the car-park.

1923
**oblique
ramps**
lingotto
giacomo matté trucco
turin

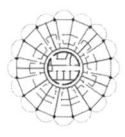

1959
**verticalism
ramps**
marina city
bertrand goldberg
chicago

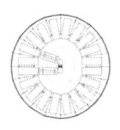

2000
**verticalism
robots**
autostadt
henn
wolfsburg

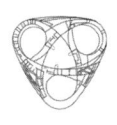

2001
**trefoil
ramps**
mercedes museum
unstudio
stuttgart

2008
**high heights
ramps**
1111 lincoln road
herzog & de meuron
miami

Carchitecture Timeline

1923

Carchitecture - Oblique

61

61 Fiat Factory, Pista del Lingotto
    Giacomo Mattè Trucco Architect Engineer
    Turin, Italy

62 Marina City
    Bertrand Goldberg Architect
    Chicago, USA

Carchitecture - Vertical

1959

62

79

2000

Carchitecture - Silo

63

63 Autostadt, Volkswagen Car Park
Henn Architekten
Wolfsburg, Germany

64 Mercedes-Benz Museum
UNStudio
Stuttgart, Germany

64

2008

Carchitecture - High Heights

65 1111 Lincoln Road
Herzog & De Meuron Architects
Miami, USA

Carchitecture - Robots

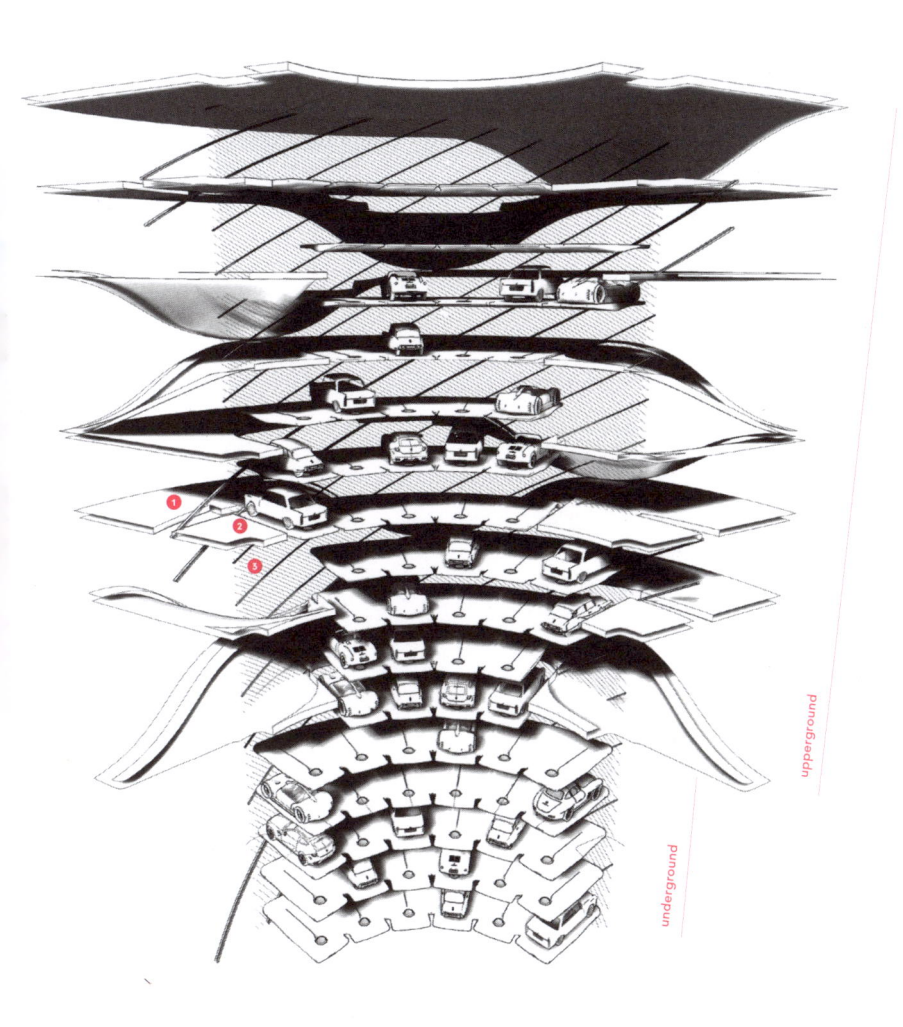

2016

① car-free surrounding nature park
② human-free car silo
③ safety fence

upperground
underground

Gran Mediterraneo, partial interior 3d sketch of the silo core

Radiant Cities

Circular and radial forms abound in the urban design history of cities. They show central organizations, horizontal planning, concentric axes, and defensive walls.
The design of a circular high-rise places the mechanical circulations at the centre of the layout.
In opposition to the radiant historical cities, where concentric axes lead to the central main building or plaza, the project unravels from its centre to its outskirts onto framed views. Namely, the Gran Mediterraneo opens panoramic views on the city. Radial and radiant ideas merge in the vertical setting to involve the mixed activities of the ideal high-rise.

84

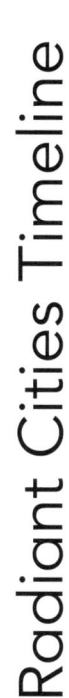

-300
hatra
iraq

1593
palmanova
italy

1624
tainan
taiwan

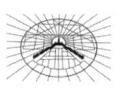

1715
karlsruhe
germany

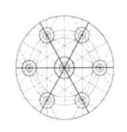

1898
garden city
uk

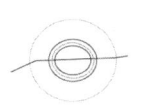

1921
nahalal
israel

1957
cern
france-switzerland

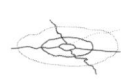

1993
city airport
usa

Radiant Cities Timeline

85 -300 Defensive Walls

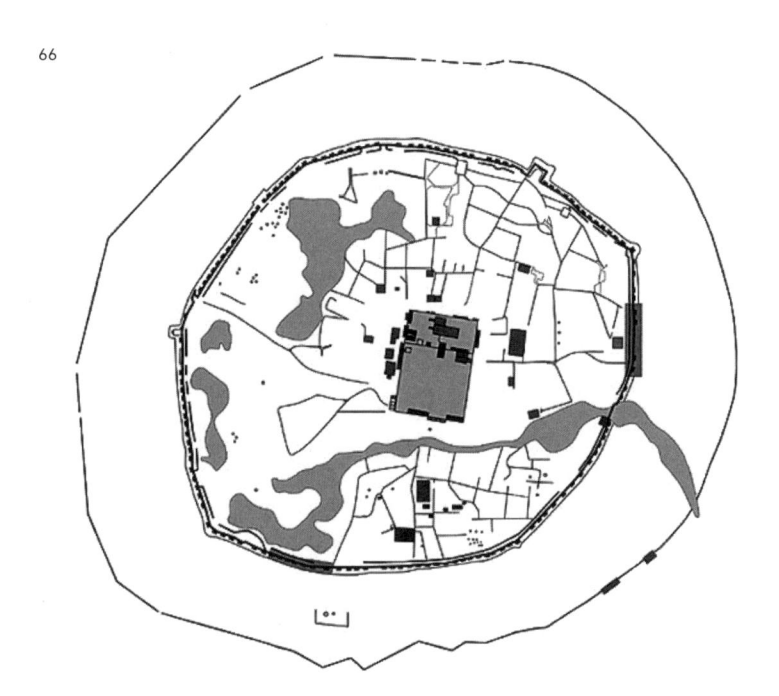

66

66 Hatra, Iraq

67 Ideal cities from the Renaissance with
the emphasis on defensive walls

Ideal City Layouts

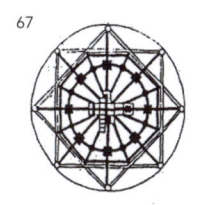

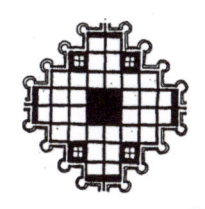

1527

67

① La Sforzinda by Filarete, 1460 – 1465
② Fra Giocondo (Giovanni of Verona), c.1433 – 1515
③ Girolamo Magi (or Maggi), c.1523 – c.1572, 1564
④ Giorgio Vasari, 1598
⑤ Antonio Lupicini, c.1530 – c.1598
⑥ Daniele Barbaro, 1513 – 1570
⑦ Pietro Cattaneo, 1537 – 1587
⑧ / ⑨ Francesco di Giorgio Martini (1439 – 1502)

1593

Ideal City

88 Radial Pattern

1721

68 Palmanova, Italy

69 Karlsruhe, Germany

1807

Defensive Walls

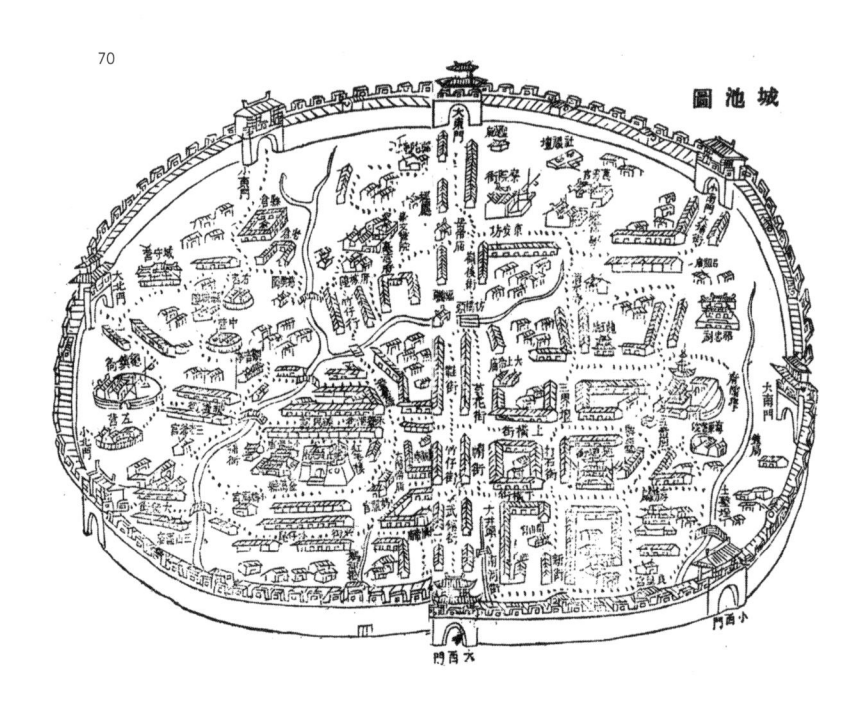

70

城池圖

70 Tainan, Taïwan

71 Garden City
United Kingdom

1898

71

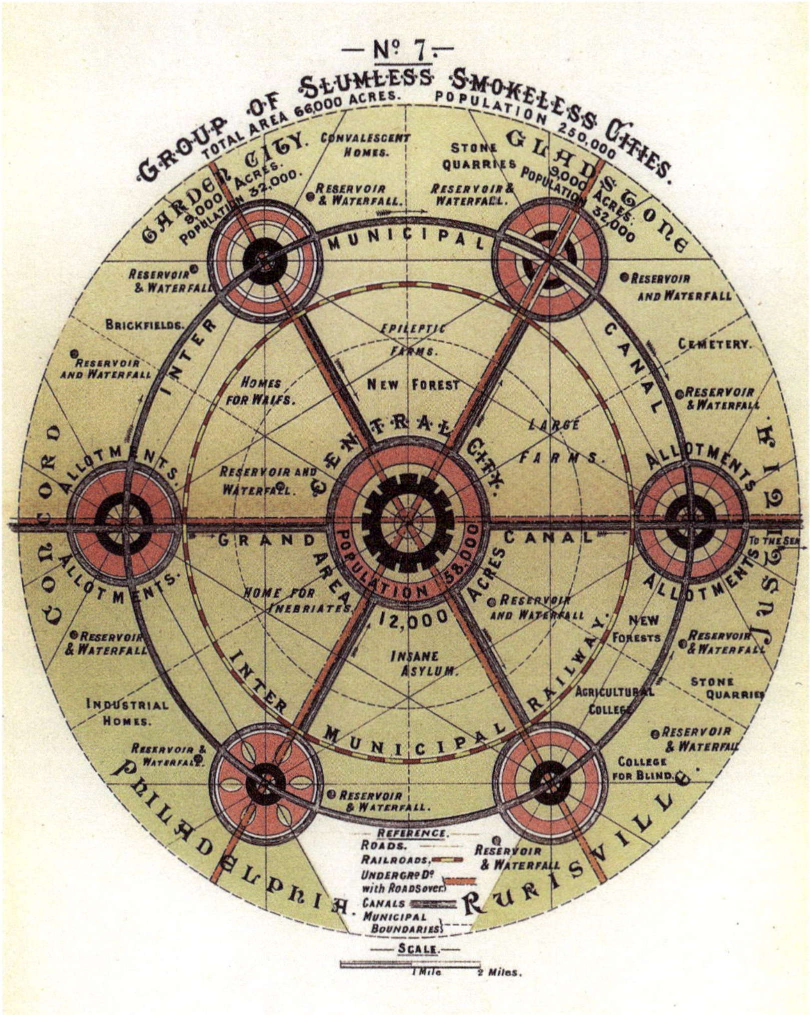
— Nº 7. —
GROUP OF SLUMLESS SMOKELESS CITIES.
TOTAL AREA 66,000 ACRES. POPULATION 250,000
GARDEN CITY. 9,000 ACRES. POPULATION 32,000.
GLADSTONE 9,000 ACRES. POPULATION 32,000
CONVALESCENT HOMES.
STONE QUARRIES
RESERVOIR & WATERFALL.
RESERVOIR & WATERFALL.
INTER MUNICIPAL CANAL
RESERVOIR & WATERFALL
RESERVOIR AND WATERFALL
BRICKFIELDS.
CEMETERY.
RESERVOIR AND WATERFALL
RESERVOIR & WATERFALL
EPILEPTIC FARMS.
HOMES FOR WAIFS.
NEW FOREST
LARGE FARMS.
CENTRAL CITY.
RESERVOIR AND WATERFALL.
ALLOTMENTS.
CONCORD
JUSTICE
GRAND CANAL
AREA 12,000 ACRES
POPULATION 58,000
TO THE SEA
HOME FOR INEBRIATES.
RESERVOIR AND WATERFALL
NEW FORESTS
RESERVOIR & WATERFALL
RESERVOIR & WATERFALL
INSANE ASYLUM.
INTER MUNICIPAL RAILWAY.
STONE QUARRIES
INDUSTRIAL HOMES.
AGRICULTURAL COLLEGE
RESERVOIR & WATERFALL
RESERVOIR & WATERFALL.
COLLEGE FOR BLIND.
RESERVOIR & WATERFALL.
PHILADELPHIA.
RURISVILLE.
REFERENCE.
ROADS.
RAILROADS.
UNDERGRD Ds with ROADS over.
CANALS
MUNICIPAL BOUNDARIES
RESERVOIR & WATERFALL
SCALE.
1 Mile 2 Miles.

1921

Farming Collectivism

72 Moshav Nahalal, Israel
Richard Kauffmann Architect

73 Particle Accelerator Complex
CERN - European Organization
for Nuclear Research, Franco - Swiss Border

Invisible Circle

1954

73

1967

Airport City

74

74 Aéroport Charles De Gaulle Terminal 1
    Paul Andreu Architect
    Roissy, France

75 Conway, USA

Airport City

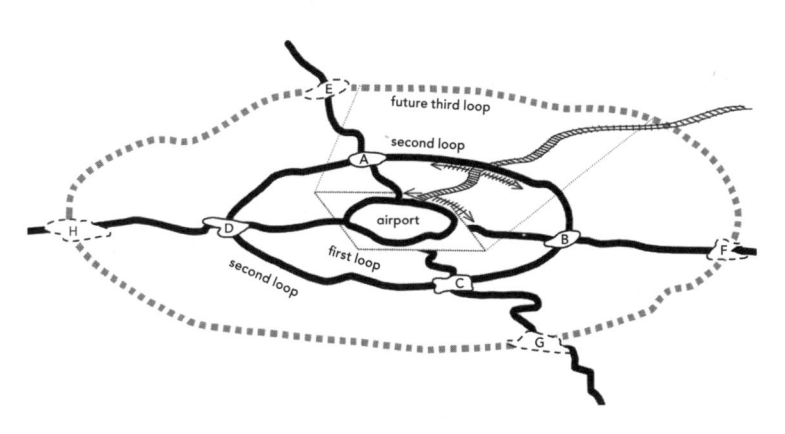

1993

75

future third loop
second loop
first loop
airport
second loop

E, A, B, C, D, F, G, H

- limited access highway
- main line rail
- commuter rail
- A,B,C,D satellite cities

Process

Vertical (Car) Park

The partly underground car-silo constitutes one-third of the high-rise. Mediterranean green nature surrounds in spiral the upper-ground automated silo. A vertical green park that is car-free and intended for pedestrians, establishes a special ground relation with the existing chosen public space. The presence of potted plants on white concrete in the Gran Mediterraneo echoes the White City's abundant green nature dangling on balconies and in-between the ground-floors of low-rise Bauhaus buildings. An Architecture-Nature relation existing in cities like Rio de Janeiro with Niemeyer's Casa das Canoas or Tokyo with Ryue Nishizawa's Garden & House.

A porous metallic fabric separates the cars from the Mediterranean green nature. Vehicles remain visible from the outside through the open-air park. Staircases in the vertical park follow the spiralling concrete topology along the metallic fence, up to a transfer floor: the hotel lobby.

The part of the tower touching the ground is not sealed with glass, showing the local nature growing on the white concrete structure. Related to the Tel Aviv's Mediterranean exterior green spaces, the Gran Mediterraneo manifests a tribute to the city's modernistic relation between concrete and nature, here in a holistic vision.

1951

Horizontal Curve

76 Tropical Nature Integrated
Casa das Canoas
Oscar Niemeyer Architect
Barra da Tijuca, Rio de Janeiro, Brazil

77 Japanese Potted Plants
Townhouse
Ryue Nishizawa Architect
Tokyo, Japan

Vertical Nature

2011

77

2016

Stepped Double Curve

① fluid steps from the double curve
② potted mediterranean nature

Potted local nature, Gran Mediterraneo, 3d sketch

Double Curve

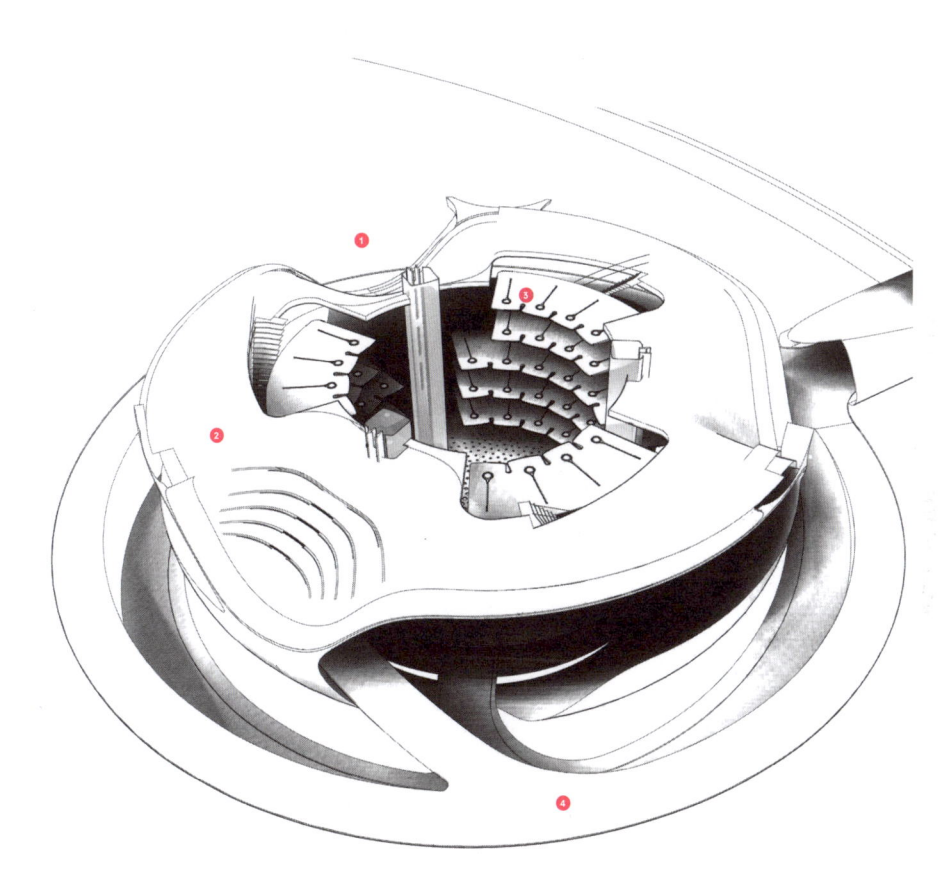

2016

1. pedestrian public space
2. car-free surrounding park
3. human-free car silo
4. underground car access

Car silo surrounded with local nature, Gran Mediterraneo, 3d sketch

1983 — Hanging Gardens

78

78 Hanging gardens of Babylon
    Parque Jaime Duque
    Tocancipa, Colombia

Local Nature - Gran Mediterraneo's car silo and spiralling park, perspective

Loci plasticity

Gran Mediterraneo is situated, as a case study, on Kikar Hamedina, the largest public space in Tel Aviv. A repetitive brutalist concrete building borders the 300 meters diameter of the pedestrian plaza. Most recent Tel Avivian high-rises are built in the vicinity of this circle, creating a concentration of skyscrapers nearby the chosen location. This neighbourhood is being gentrified as the ground floors of the surrounding brutalist buildings welcome luxury shops, and the upper floors become expensive to afford. The circular plaza was designed in the 1970s by Oscar Niemeyer who proposed curvy buildings and a high-rise on the circle, which remained unbuilt. Several projects have been proposed since then, including a recent proposal of three residential towers and a park. Nothing has been built so far. A social protest in 2011 gathered 1 million of people on the Kikar Hamedina, which is symbolic, as a void in the city.

Site Case Study Timeline

1960
circuses

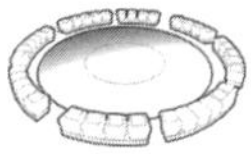

1970
oscar niemeyer
built

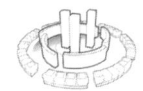

1970
oscar niemeyer
unbuilt

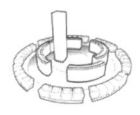

1970
oscar niemeyer
unbuilt

1970
contractor hochzeit
unbuilt

2001
international competition
unbuilt

2009
international competition
unbuilt

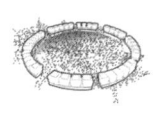

2011
social protest

2012
luxury retail roundabout

1960

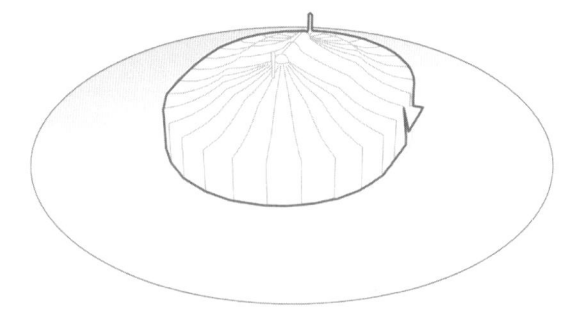

Kikar Hamedina

Circuses

Kikar Hamedina

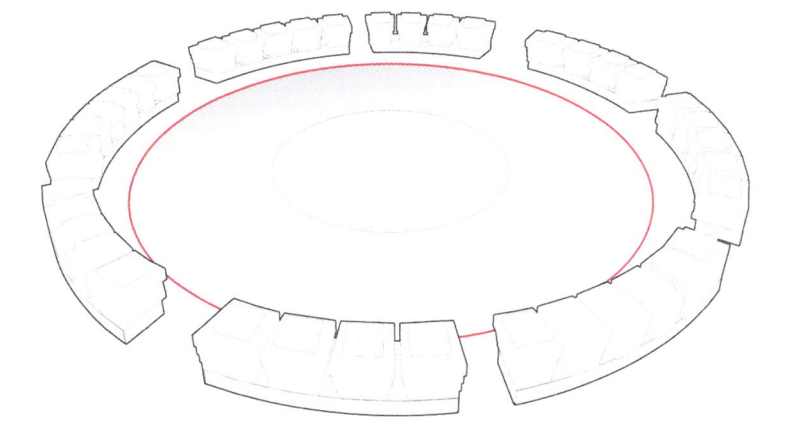

1970

Largest plaza in the city
Diameter 290 m
Housing buildings: Abba Elhanani Architect
Hamedina Circle: Abba Elhanani,
Yisrael Lotan & Oscar Niemeyer Architects

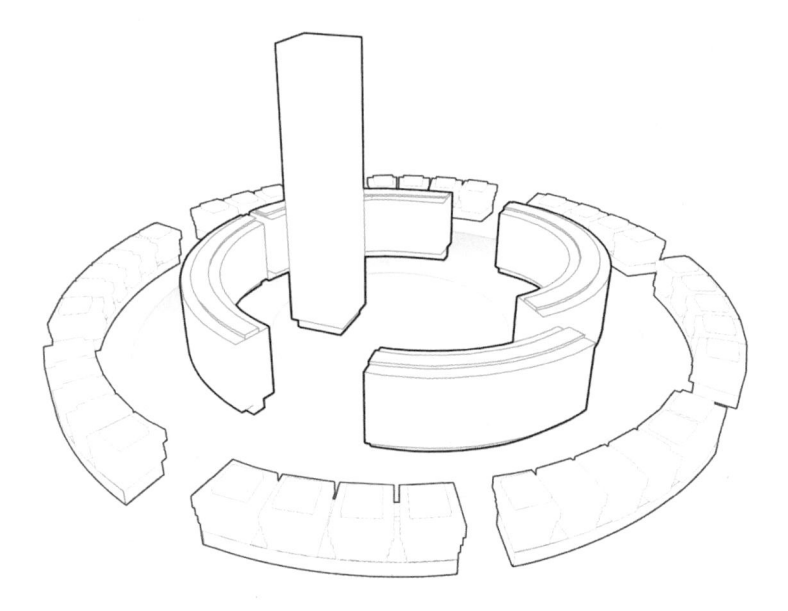

Kikar Hamedina

One high-rise and four curvy low-rises
Unbuilt, Oscar Niemeyer Architect

110   Kikar Hamedina   1970

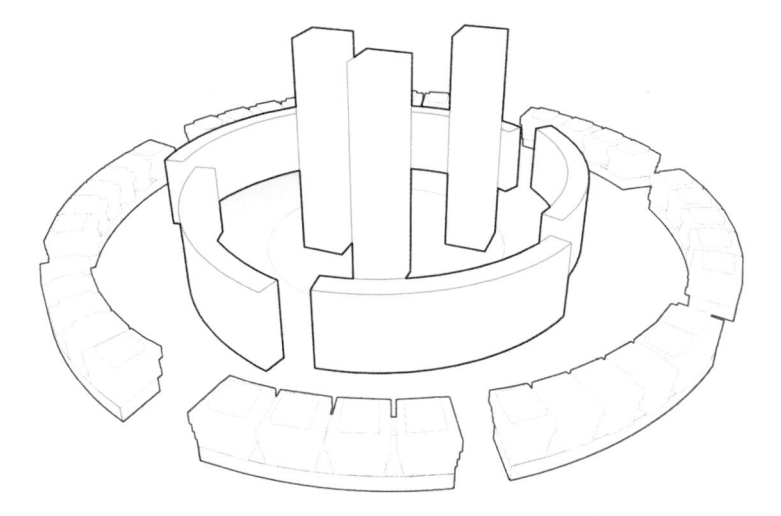

Three high-rises and five curvy low-rises
Unbuilt, Oscar Niemeyer Architect

111

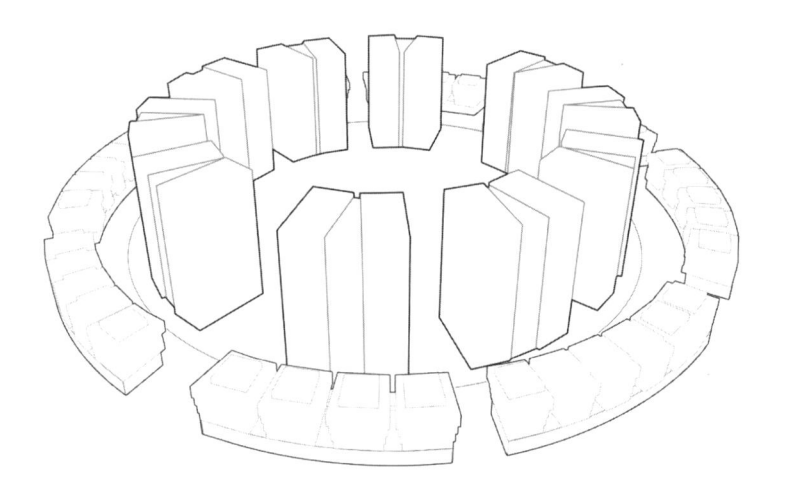

1970

Kikar Hamedina

Ten high-rises
Unbuilt, Contractor Hochzeit

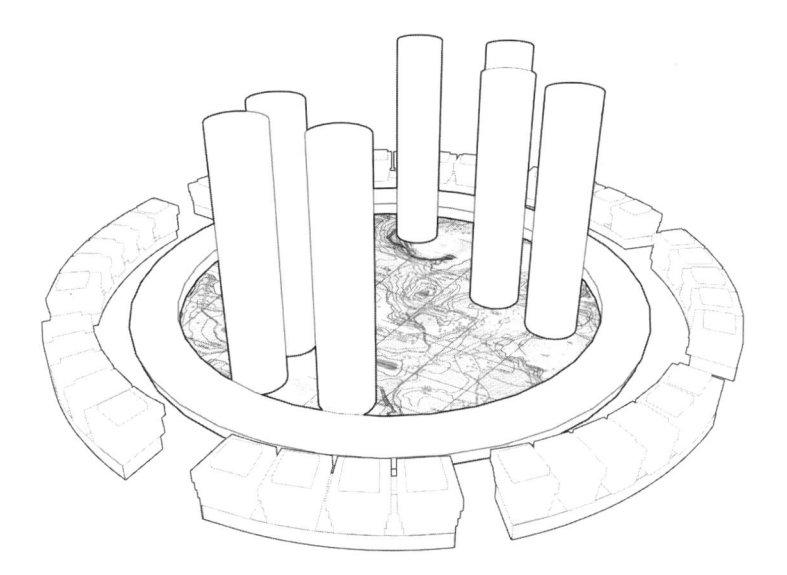

Kikar Hamedina

2001

International architecture competition
Unbuilt, Ateliers Jean Nouvel

2009

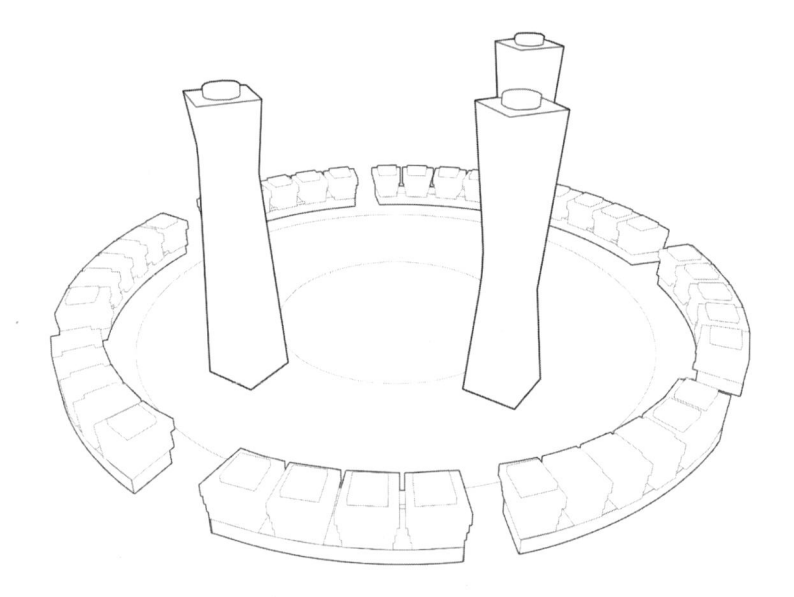

Kikar Hamedina

Controversial international architecture competition
Winning entry, Unbuilt, MYS Architects

114 Kikar Hamedina 2011

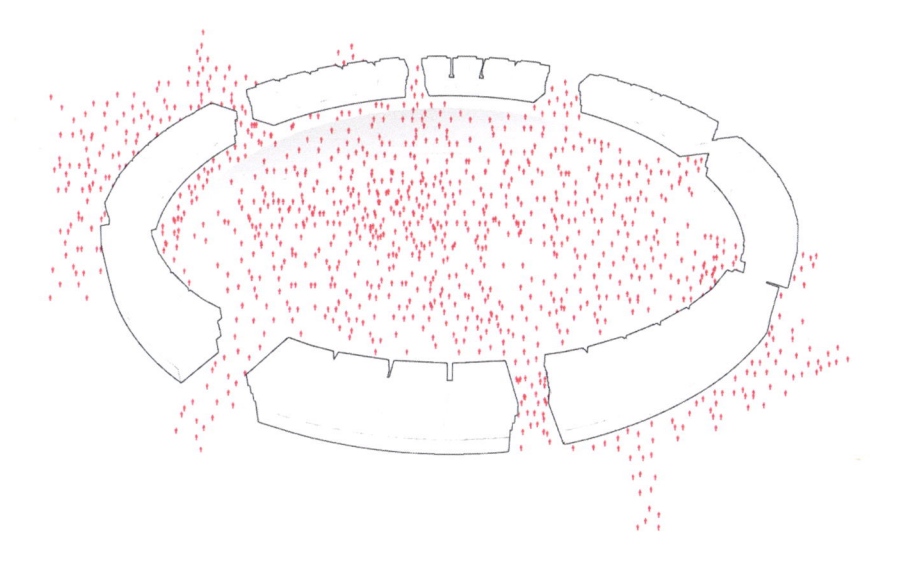

March of the Million
Demonstration for social justice

2012 — Kikar Hamedina

Luxury retail roundabout and gentrification

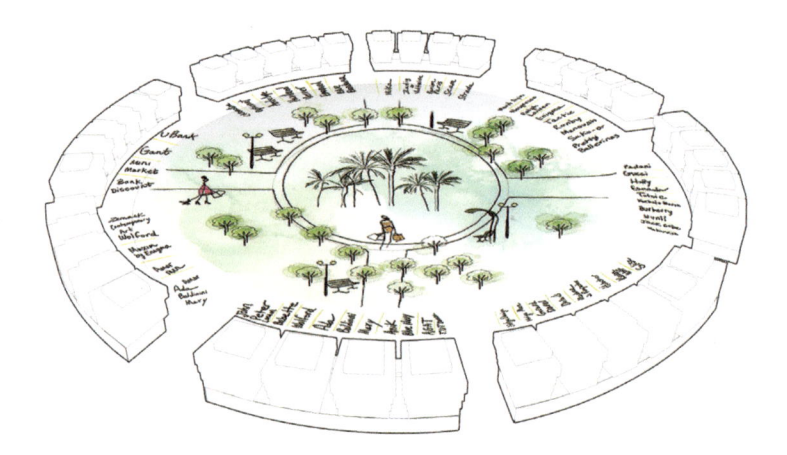

Kikar Hamedina

2012

79

79 Housing buildings: Abba Elhanani Architect
    Hamedina Circle: Abba Elhanani, Yisrael Lotan &
    Oscar Niemeyer Architects

Circular Landscape Urbanism

Gran Mediterraneo is carefully positioned at the south-eastern side of the pedestrian circle Kikar Hamedina to maximize hours of shadow on the plaza, and let free the views crossing at the centre of the public space. Vehicles access the Gran Mediterraneo's silo by a new subterranean ramp.
The ground treatment of the Plaza is inspired by the circular geometries of the high-rise, the Arabic patterns found in Jaffa's arts and crafts and the saltworks in Niger.
To reinforce the physical limits of the Plaza as well as the pedestrian continuity with the city, peripheries of the roundabout have been elevated as circular inclined ramps. These elevated ramps include a vehicle access to the tower's basement, a theatre and a local supermarket.

118 Circular Groundscraper 1971

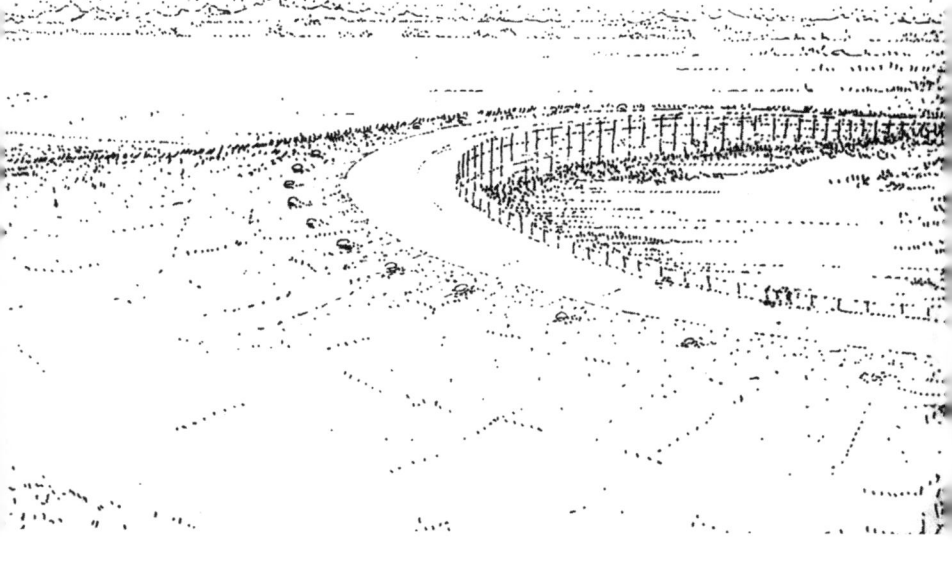

80

80 Unità Residenziale Ovest Olivetti
Roberto Gabetti and Aimaro Isola Architects, with Luciano Re
Ivrea, Italy

2015

Circular Accessible Roof

81

81 Fuji Kindergarten
    Tezuka Architects
    Tokyo, Japan

120   Transforming Kikar Hamedina   2016

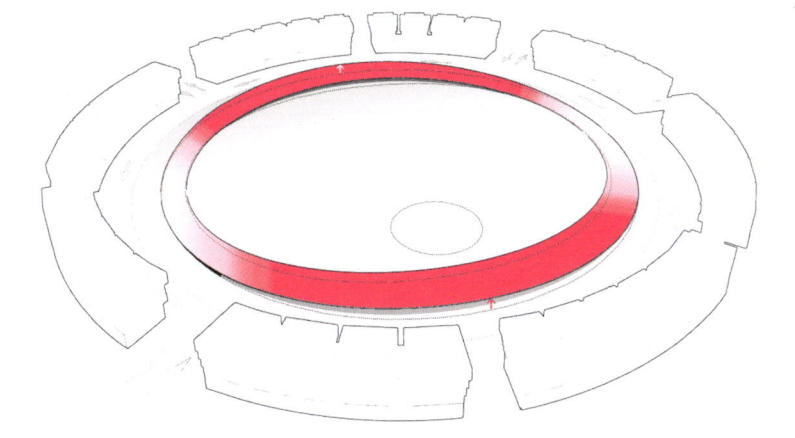

Gyratory inclined public space

121

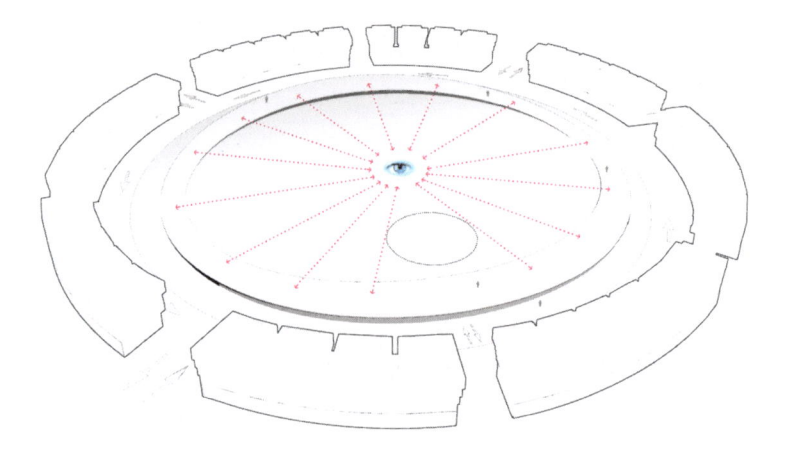

2016

Transforming Kikar Hamedina

Elevated amphitheatrical park

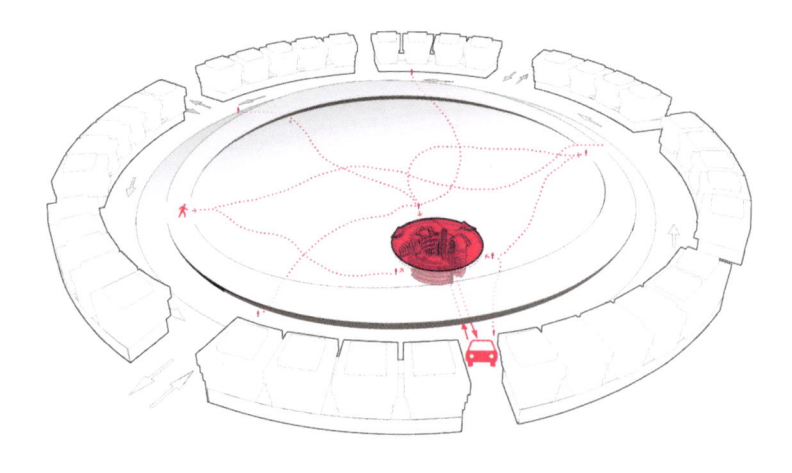

Subterranean car access and pedestrian plaza

Transforming Kikar Hamedina

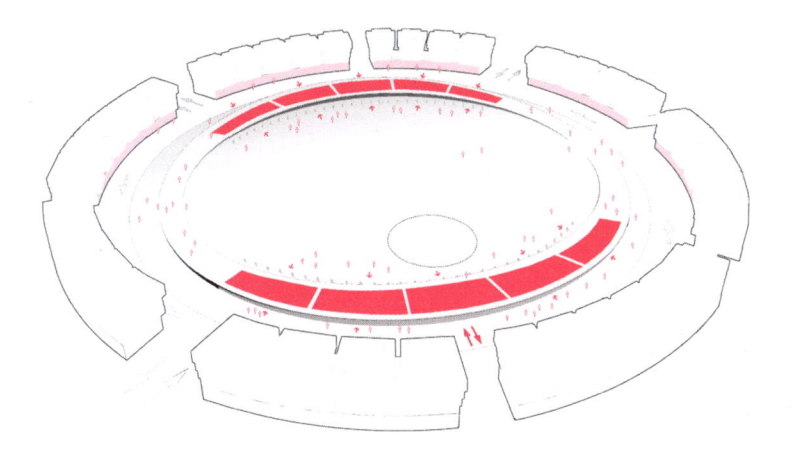

2016

Shops and terraces

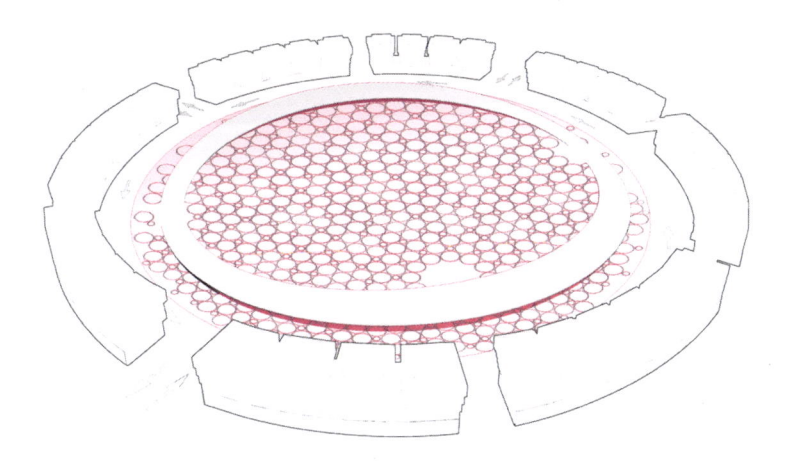

Ground arabesque

Niger Saltworks

82 Man-made ground circular patterns in Teguidda-n-Tessoumt

83 Double cover of hexagonal packing over two marked circles

83

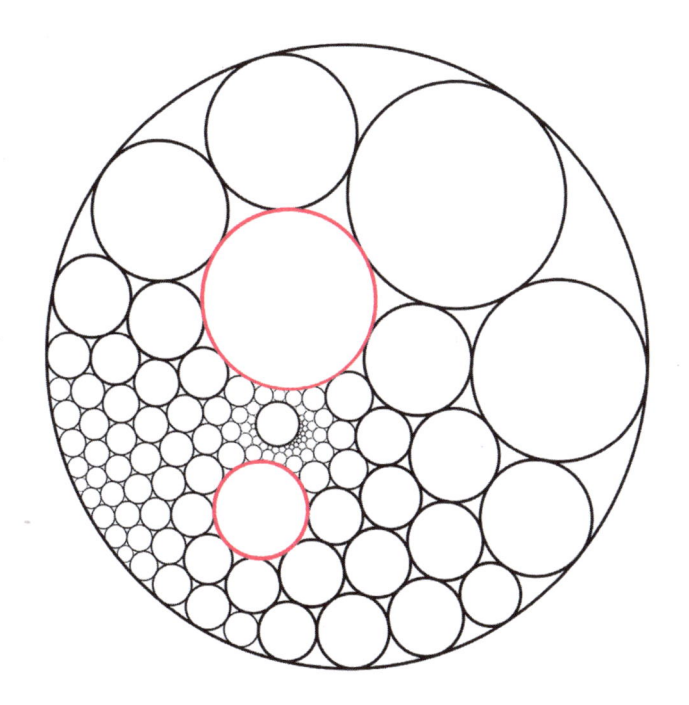

125   2016   Transforming Kikar Hamedina

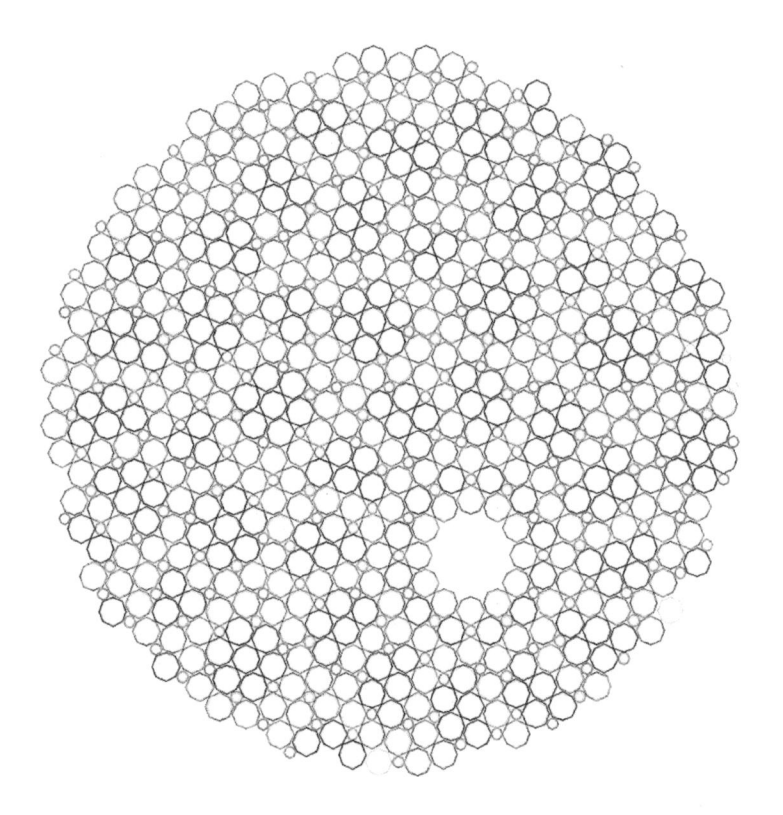

Parametrical circle packing forming
a ground arabesque
Radial circles proliferation starting from
the high-rise location

126 Transforming Kikar Hamedina 2016

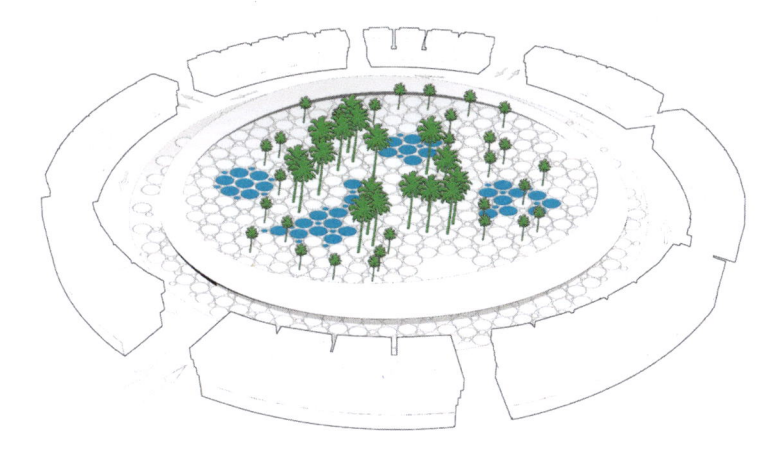

Existing and relocated trees with additional puddles of water

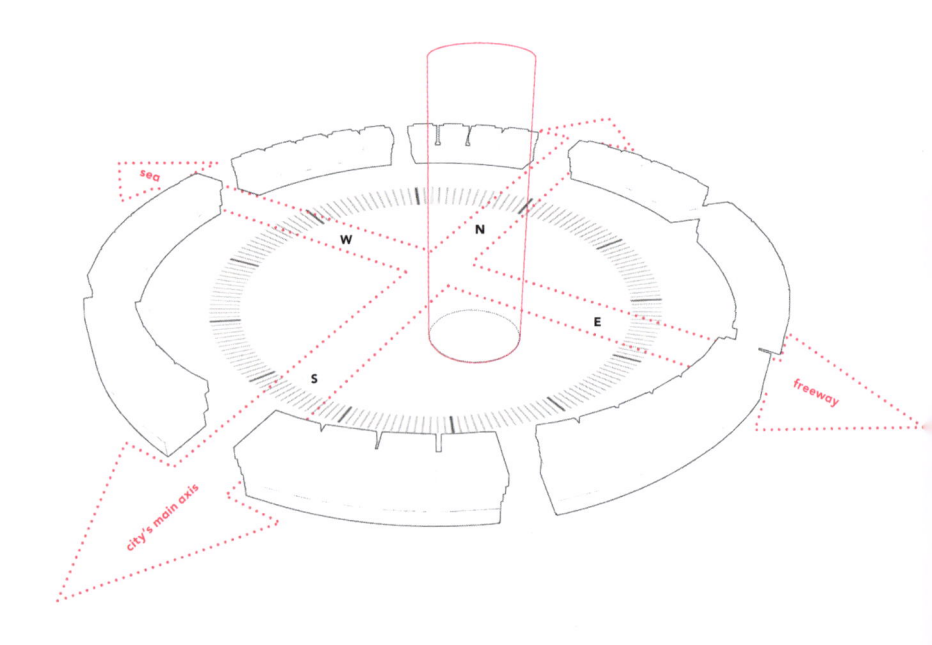

127   **2016**   Locating the Gran Mediterraneo

South-east location

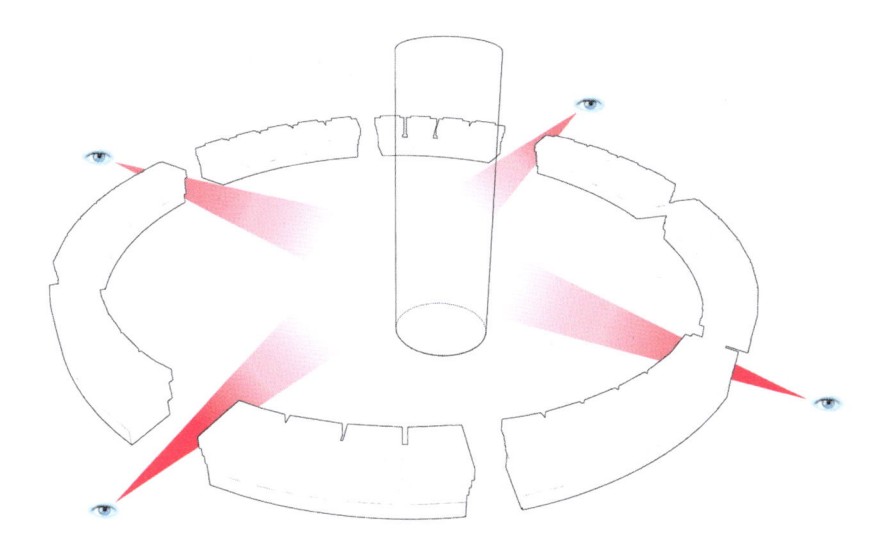

128 Locating the Gran Mediterraneo 2016

Main lines of crossing views preserved

2016

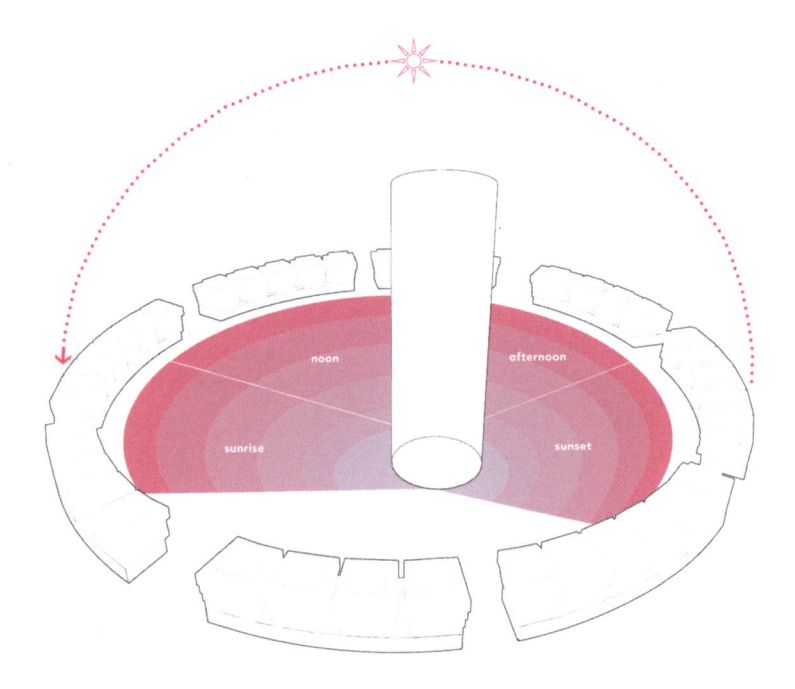

Locating the Gran Mediterraneo

Sun run on the proposal maximizing shadows on the plaza

Mixed Use High-Rise

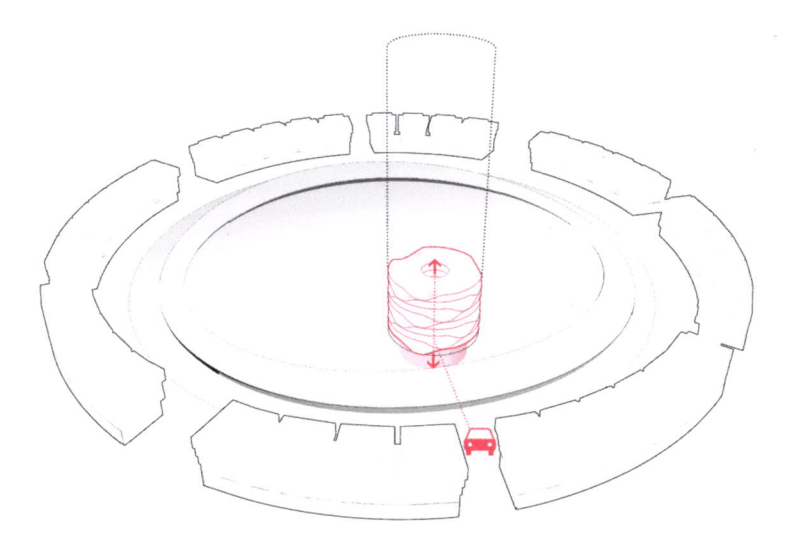

Automated car-park silo and spiralling Mediterranean park

Mixed-Use High-Rise

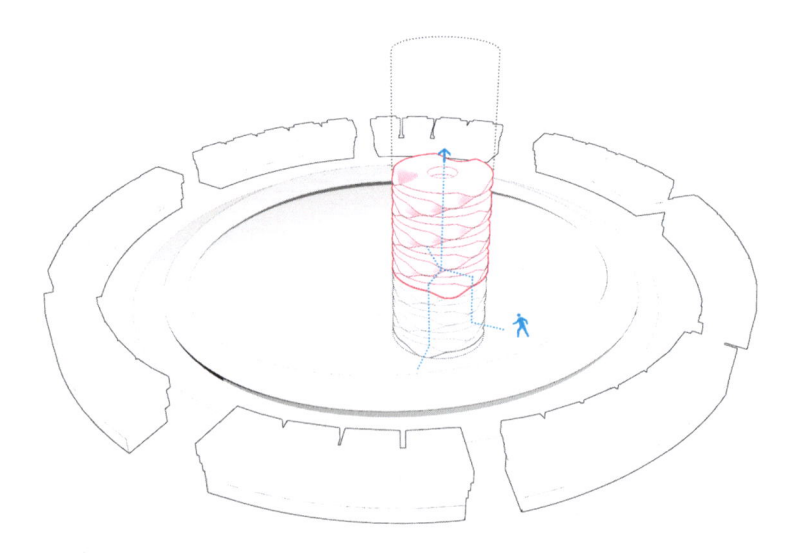

Panoramic hotel

Vertical kibbutz

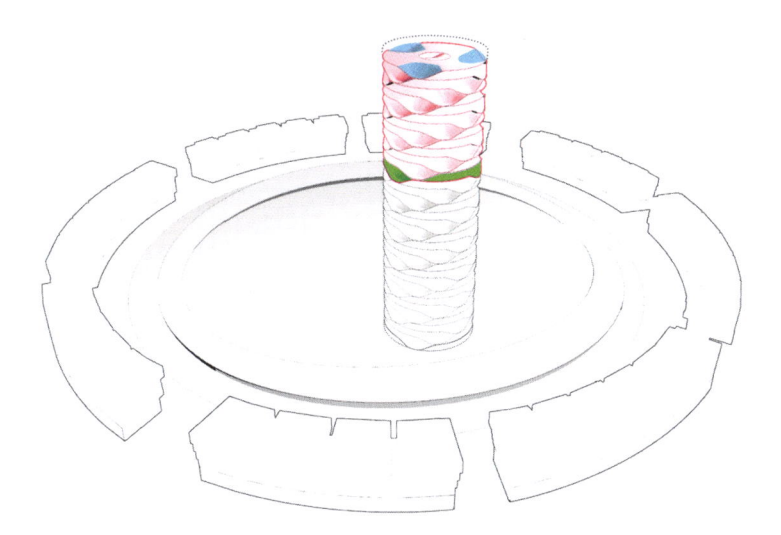

Endlessness

Gran Mediterraneo is defined by the superposition of a similar rotating and distorted concrete slab. These stacked slabs, revealing a spiral effect from the exterior, are generated by the repetition of a geometrically optimized topology. Impossible spaces and a feeling of infinity constitute the genesis of the vertical design. Defining from the beginning an architectural design that will be a vertical translation of "reaching the sky" is the basic idea underlying a vertical structure. Working on the skyscraper's design, inventing a specific topology based on the distortion of a circular concrete slab, allows the creation of an infinite double-curved and mathematical space for living and parking.

The Möbius Strip and the Klein Bottle, two mathematical figures of impossible spaces, are at the origins and the fundamentals of the architectural language illustrated in the following pages of this chapter. Several architects have used topologies, shells, and vaults, working on the double curvature, and constantly showing how to go beyond the squared grid of the Cartesian Space, while optimizing engineering design with materials like Concrete, Earth, Stone, Metal, and Wood, improving the resistance of Arches by compression, and reducing the quantity of Matter.

Curves and double-curved spaces are also the fundamentals of the Gran Mediterraneo plasticity. The project aims to shake up and challenge the re-thinking of the current vertical construction pattern in Tel Aviv, by offering more sensuality, specificity and personality inside the high-rises living spaces. The topological structure defines both the external aesthetics as well as the inner spaces. Exterior and Interior are one. There would be no need for additional "interior design" to "decorate" the Gran Mediterraneo.

1858

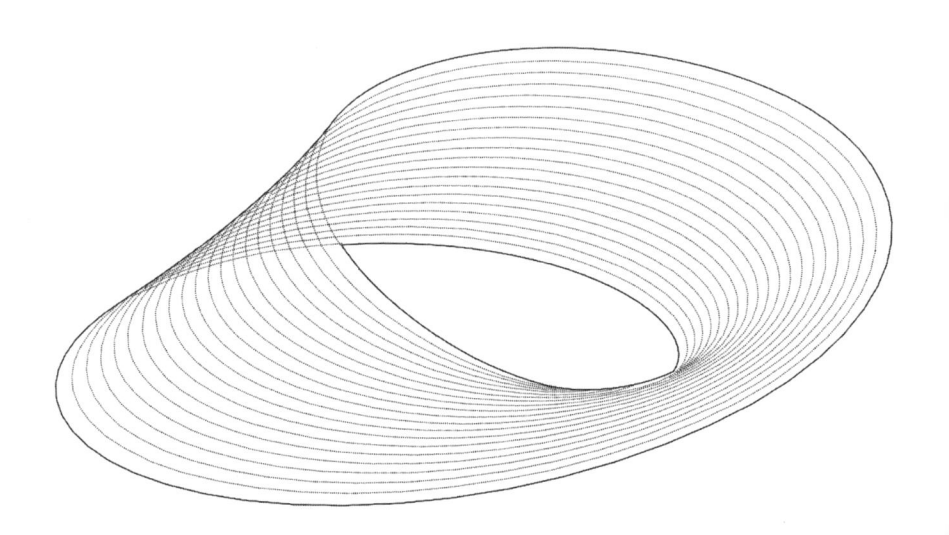

Topologies

84

84 Möbius Strip

85 Klein Bottle

Topologies

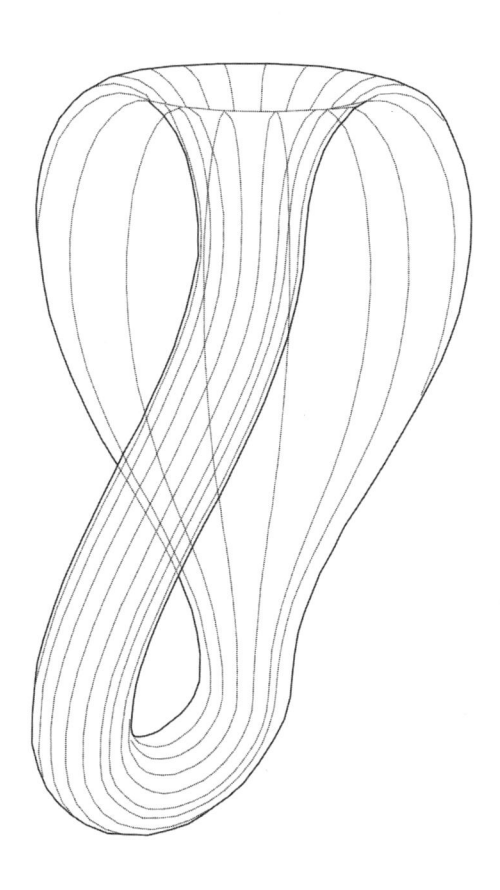

85

1955

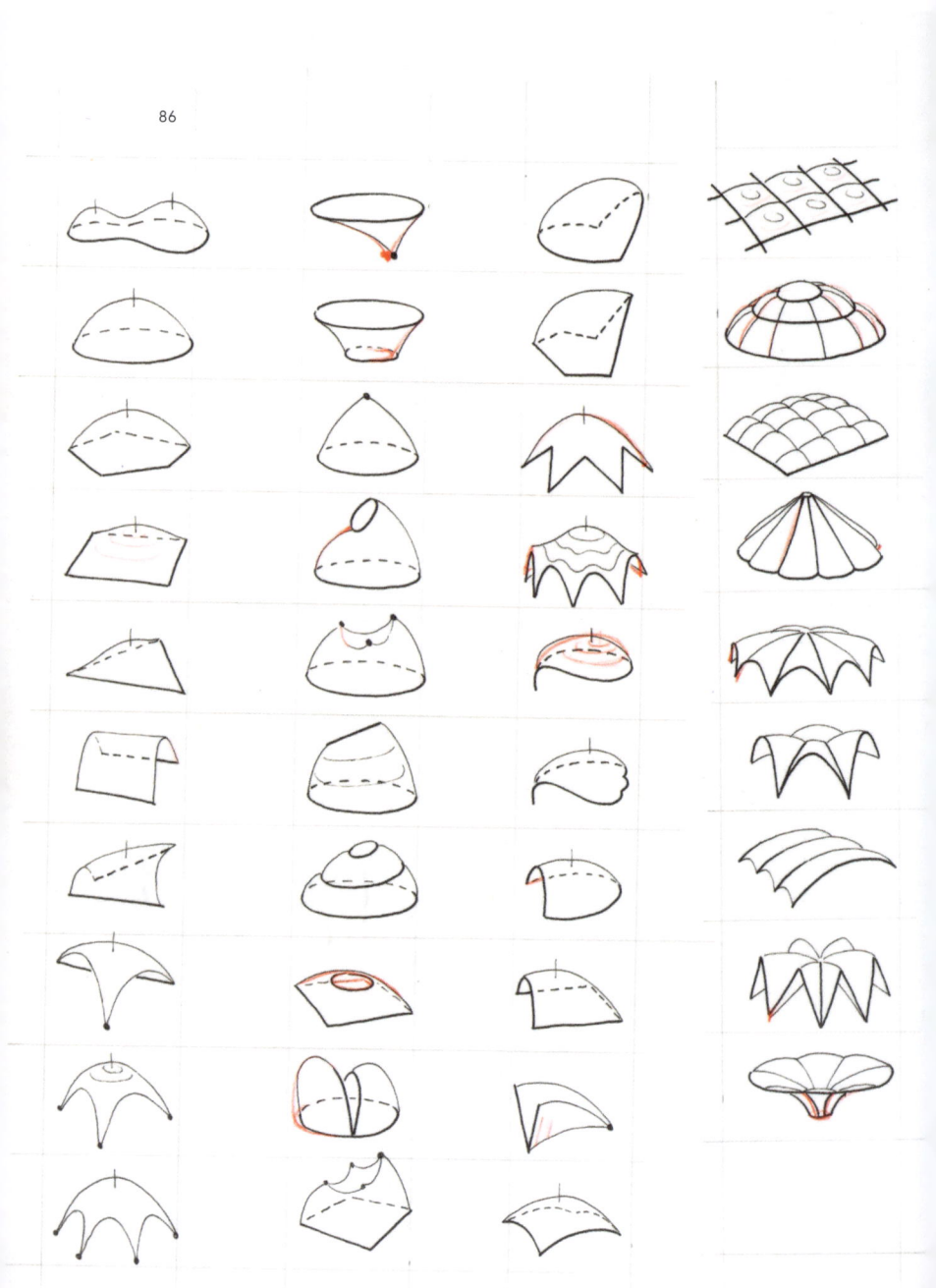

Concrete Shells

86

Concrete Shells

1958

87

86 Natural Hills
   Preparatory sketches
   Heinz Isler

87 Restaurant Los Manantiales
   Félix Candela Outeriño Architect
   Xochimilco, Mexico

139 1959　　　　　　　Endlessness

88

88　Frederick Kiesler
　　Model for an "Endless House"
　　New York

89　Tour Sans Fins
　　Jean Nouvel & Associés
　　Paris, France
　　Winning Competition, Unbuilt

Endlessness

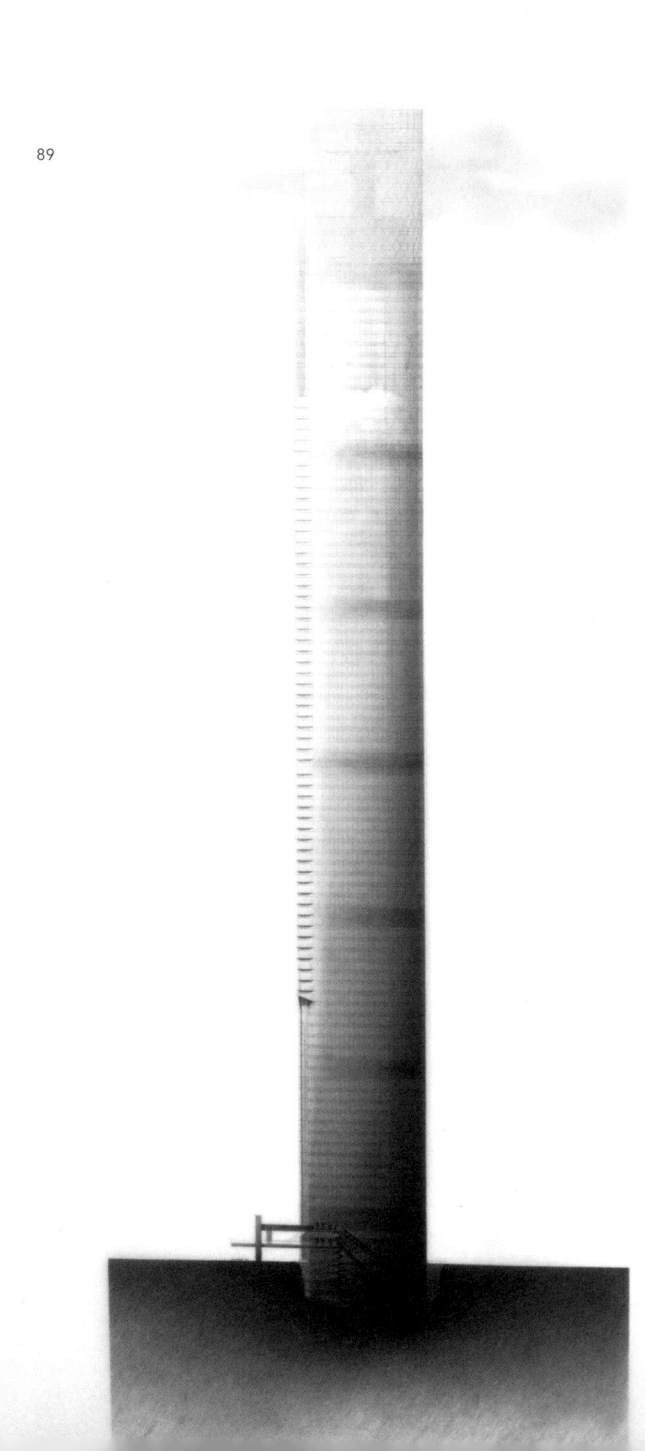

1989

89

Topologies

90

90 Möbius House
    UNStudio
    't Gooi, the Netherlands

91 Meiso no Mori Municipal Funeral Hall
    Toyo Ito & Associates Architects
    Kakamigahara, Gifu, Japan

91

143

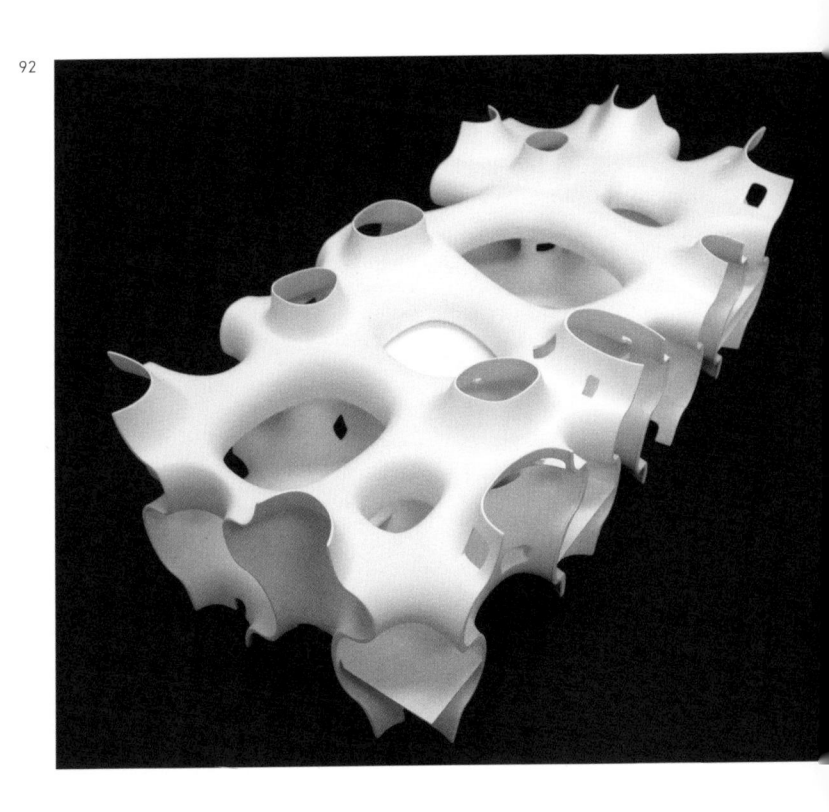

2009

Topologies

92

92 National Taichung Theater
    Toyo Ito & Associates Architects
    Taïwan

93 Villa Ypsilon
    Lassa Architects
    Finikounda, Greece

94 Earth Blocks Vaults: Prototype Droneport Shell
    The Norman Foster Foundation with Future Africa
    EPFL and Ochsendorf, DeJong & Block with Block
    Research Group, ETH Zurich
    Venice, Italy

144 Shells & Vaults 2015-6

93

94

Form Finding

The process of form finding and visualization of ideas for Gran Mediterraneo started with several and separated fields of investigations: Spatial Structures, Envelopes, Circulatory Systems, and Ecosystems. Each field of research was used separately in the design to experiment and discover innovative elements of a singular architectural language. The separate investigations were then progressively combined and negotiated, in terms of hierarchy, in an architectural synthesis, by means of hand sketches, physical models, and drawings.
This approach of design places intuition, experimentation and form prior to function and location, a design methodology taught by David Tajchman.

"Futures From Natures" is a teaching methodology of Architectural Design based on inspirations to be found in other realms of life than Architecture. Developed by David Tajchman since 2009, as a teaching brief in several schools of architecture in Europe, Asia, Northern and

[146] Southern America, the methodology has demonstrated its unique qualities of an innovative process for form production, using natures as inexhaustible resources for inspiration, and their translation into architectural elements by "making".

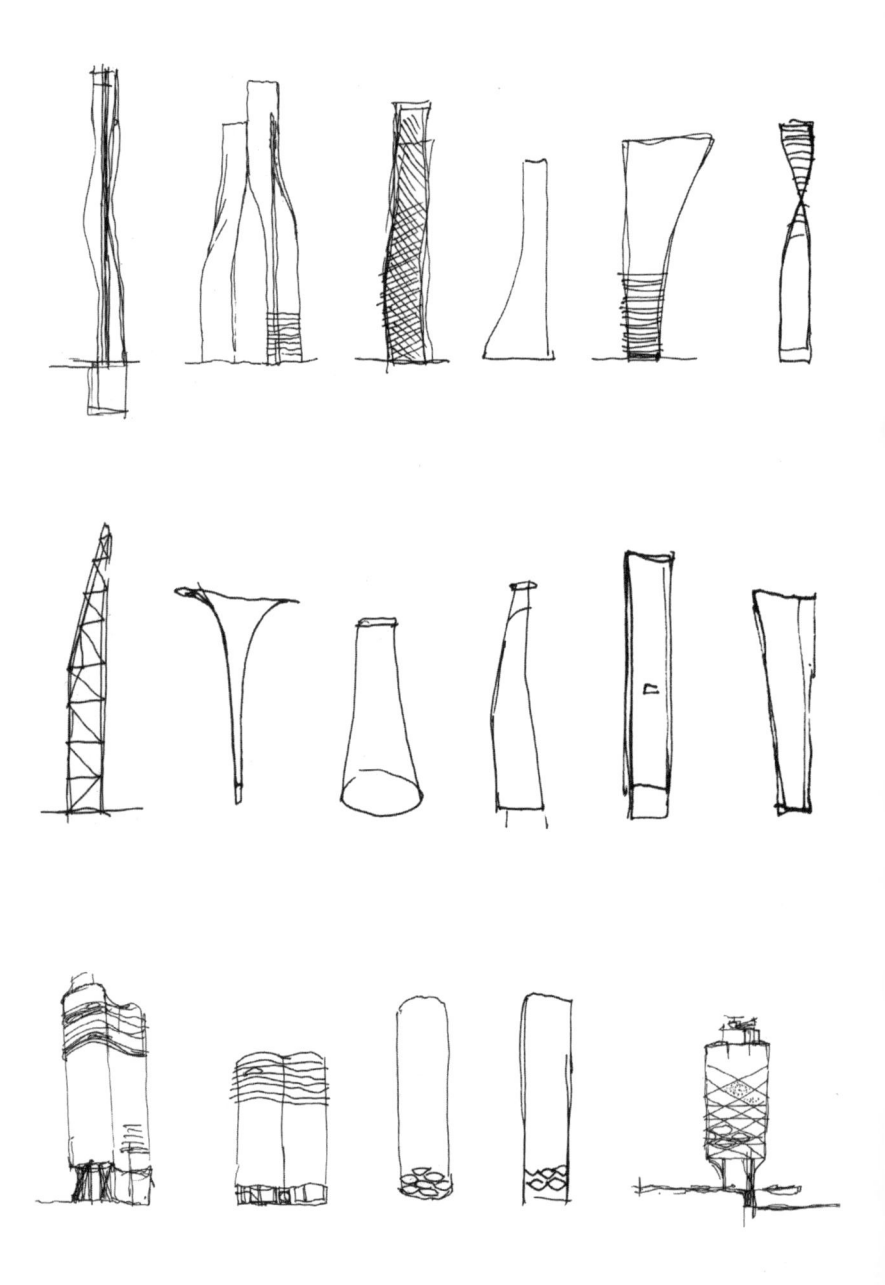

Silhouette

148 Form Finding

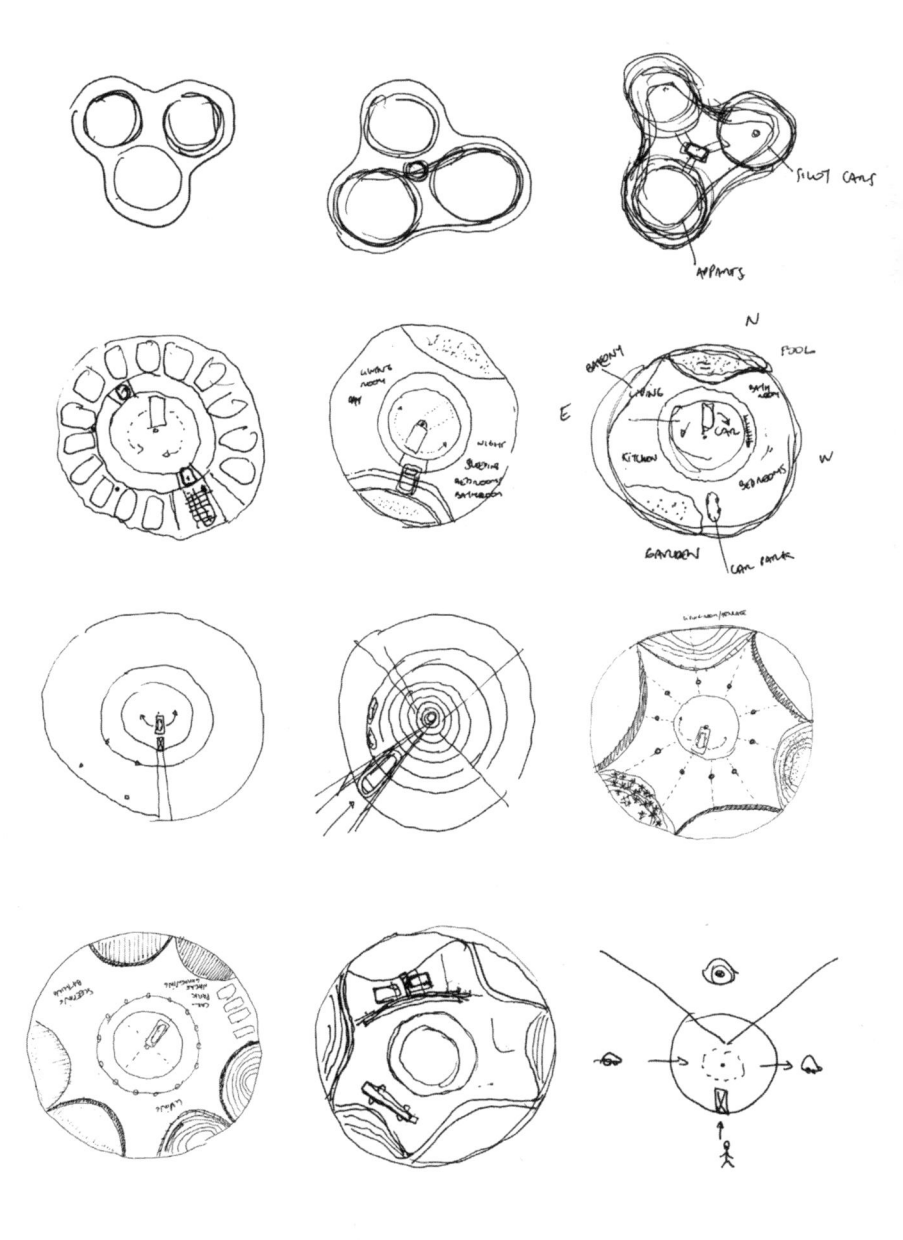

Function follows topology

149   Form Finding

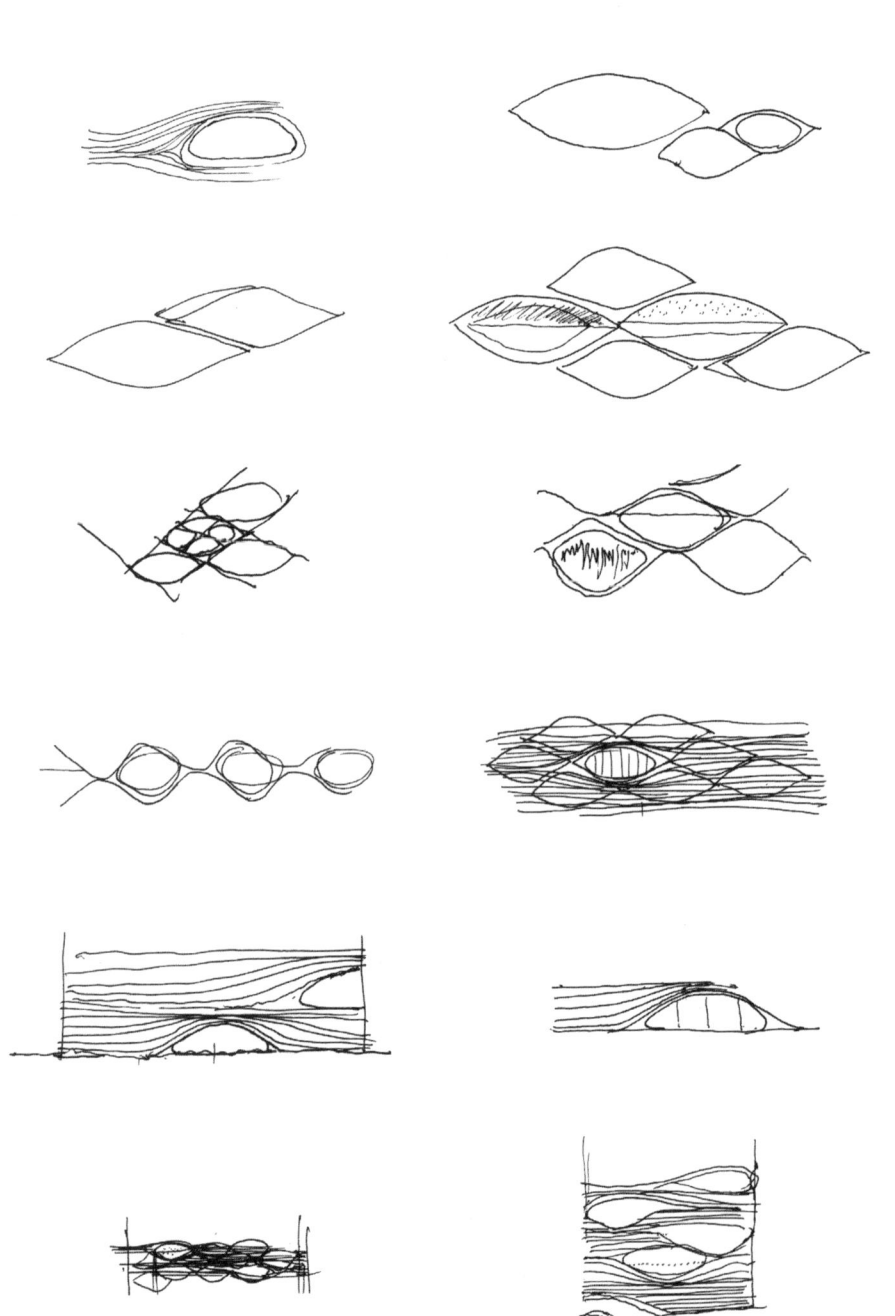

Morphogenesis

Topology

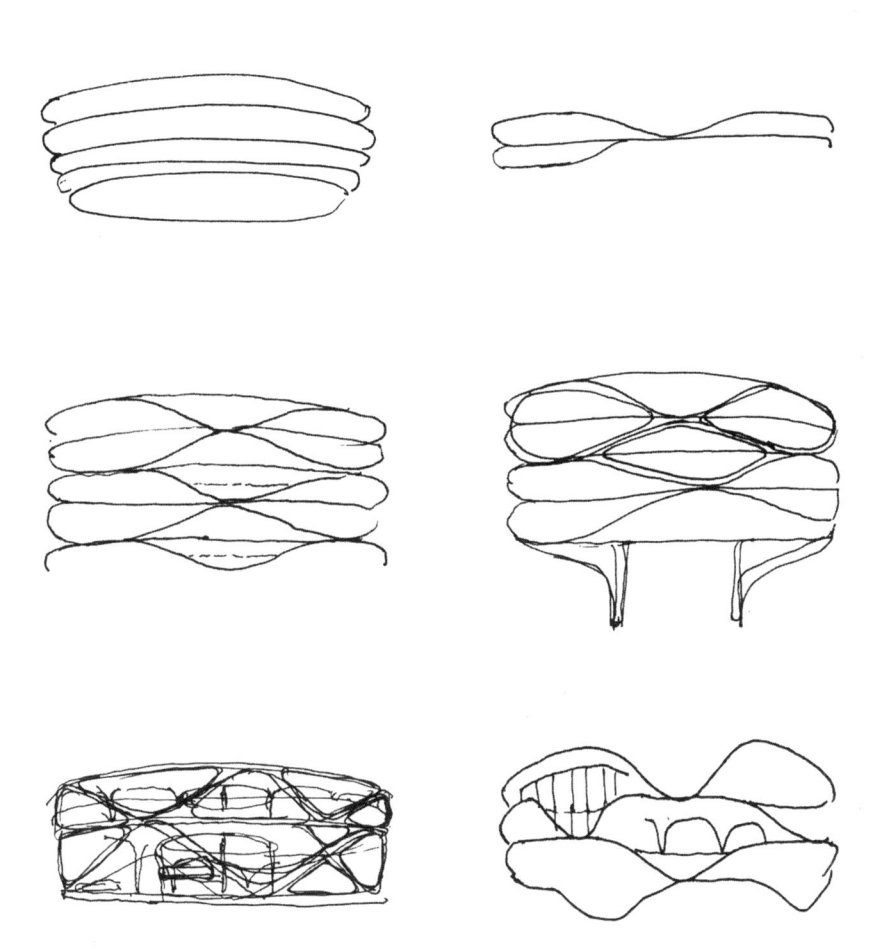

Mediterranean topology for inspiration

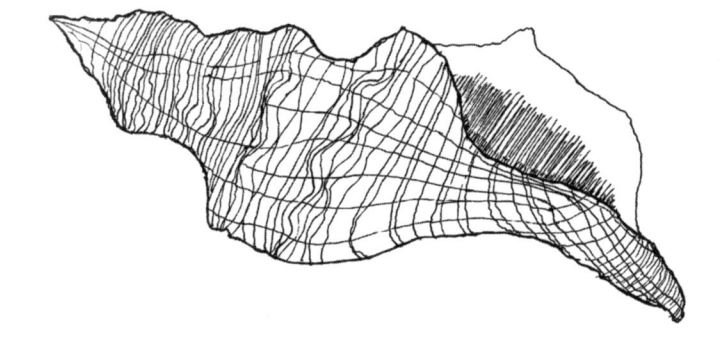

Topology

Topology

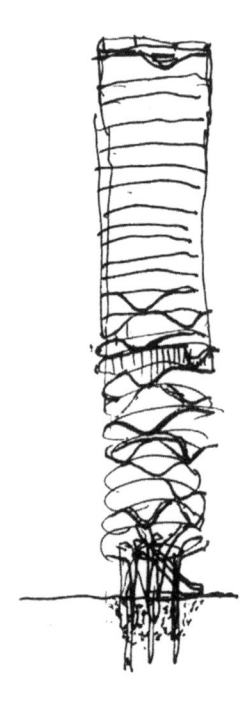

Topology

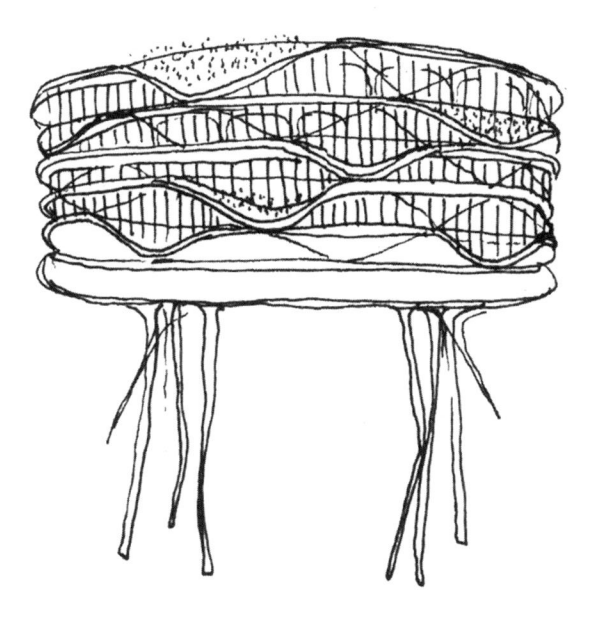

155 Form Finding

Handcrafted model, plumb sheet

Handcrafted model, plumb sheet

Progress

Digital Translation

We believe in a mix of artisanal savoir-faire and digital fabrication. The visual inspirations from natures are translated into schematic handmade physical models and mathematical figures with the help of the computer.

The association of handcrafting and computer assisted design belongs to the contemporary and future ways of building. The digital translation allows us to detail and maintain the complexity of our ideas, when hands cannot always accurately achieve the visualization and the tuning of the infinite spaces developed in the Gran Mediterraneo. Digital three-dimensional documents replace the traditional two-dimensional drawings, as such topologies cannot be illustrated here in two dimensions. Nowadays, building companies use the same digital technologies as designers, architects, and engineers to construct complex geometries. The Gran Mediterraneo will be built with fiber reinforced concrete, casted in formworks pre-fabricated in workshops through rapid manufacturing technologies.

Tower Of Babel

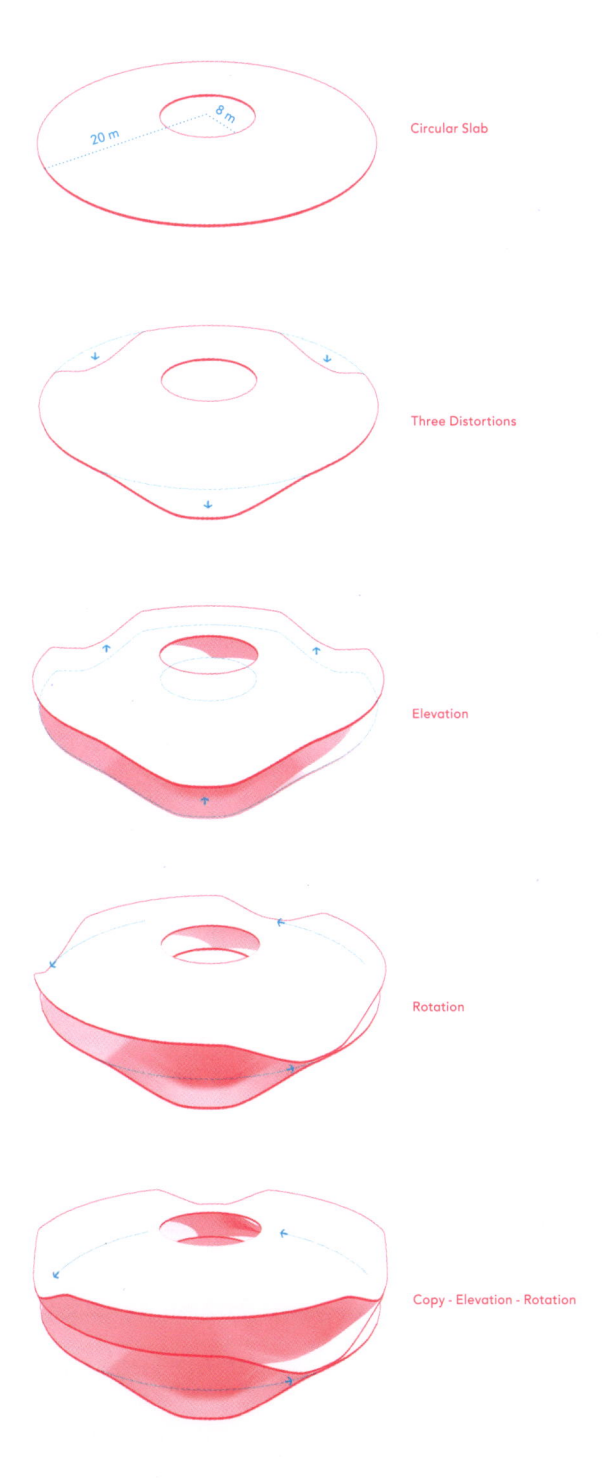

Circular Slab

Three Distortions

Elevation

Rotation

Copy - Elevation - Rotation

Vertical Topology

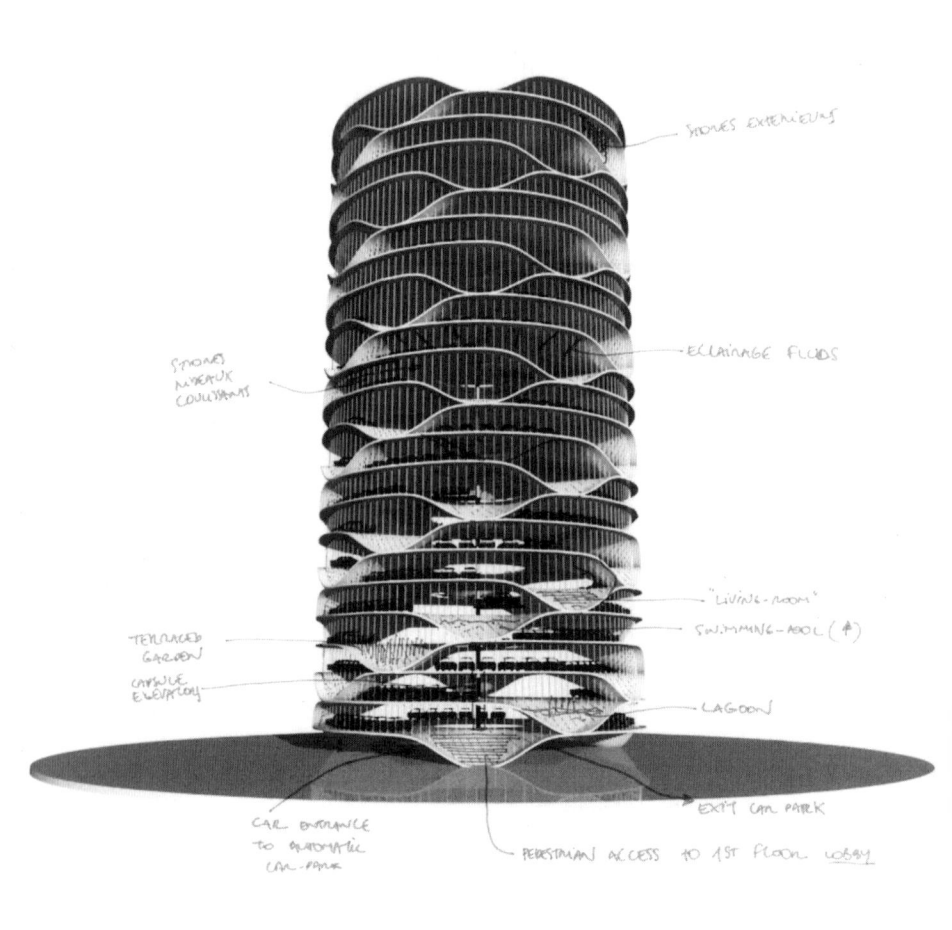

First digital synthesis visualization, 3d sketch

Research on a controlled variation of distorted slabs in relation with the Kikar Hamedina

Radial Automated Car-Park

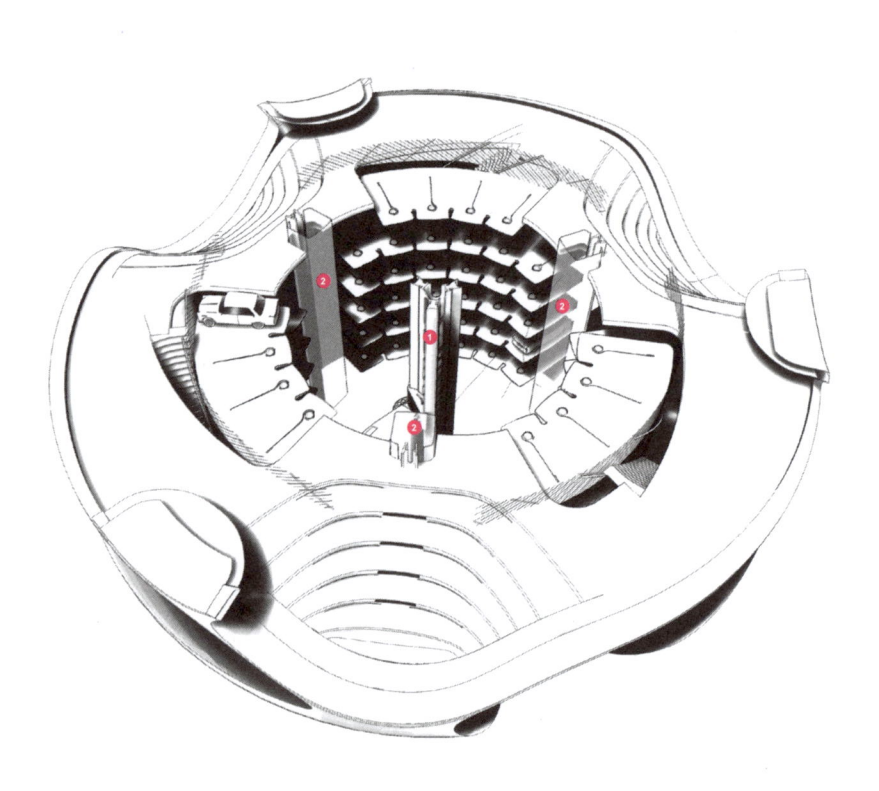

1. automated platform for vehicles
2. human elevators

Separate elevators for cars and humans

Radial Automated Car-Park

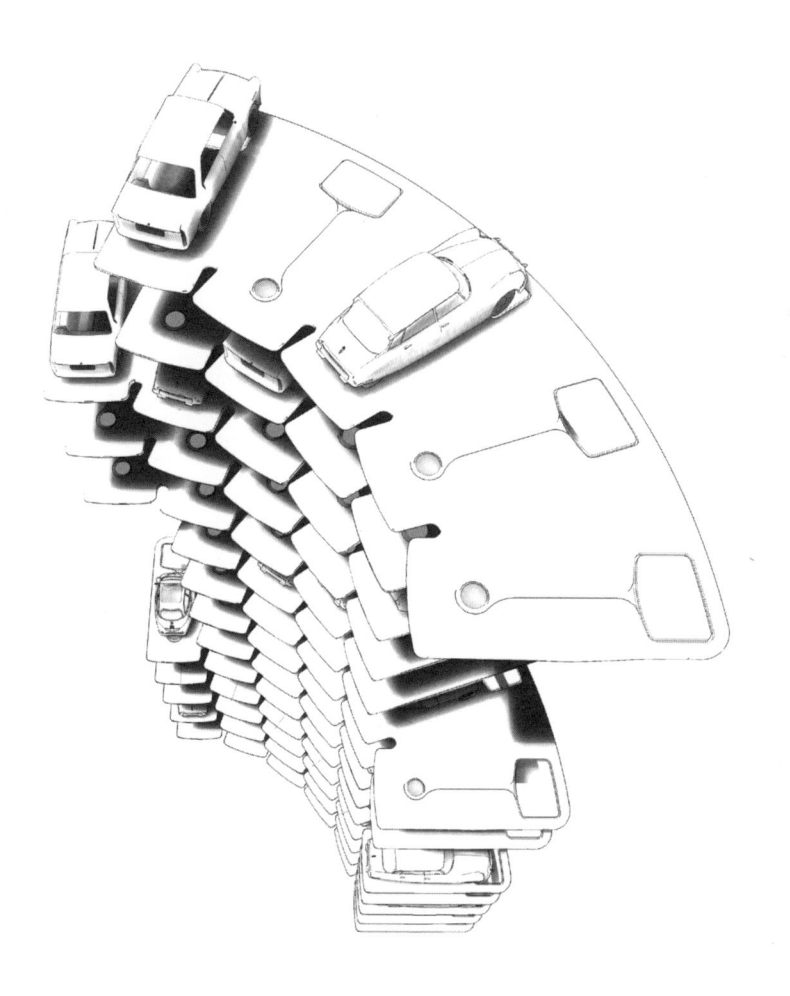

Optimizing parking spaces

Radial Automated Car-Park

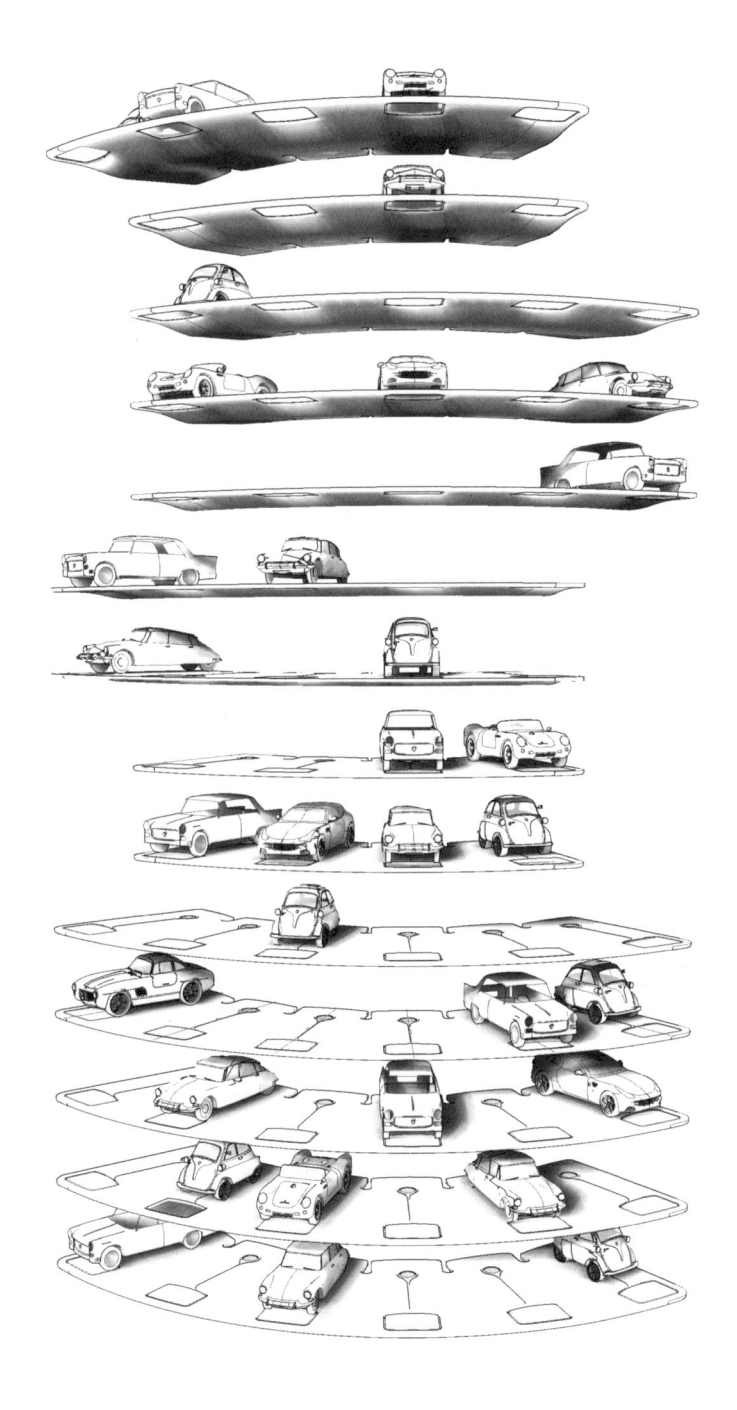

Optimizing parking spaces

Radial Automated Car-Park

automated platform for vehicles

capsule elevator

Elevators

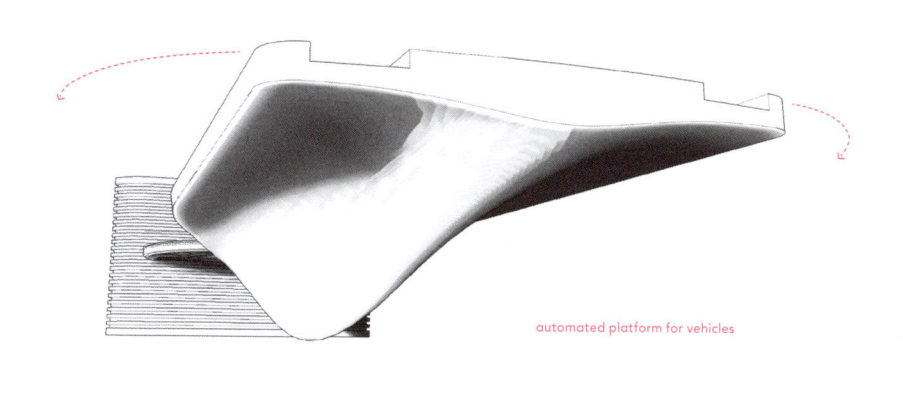

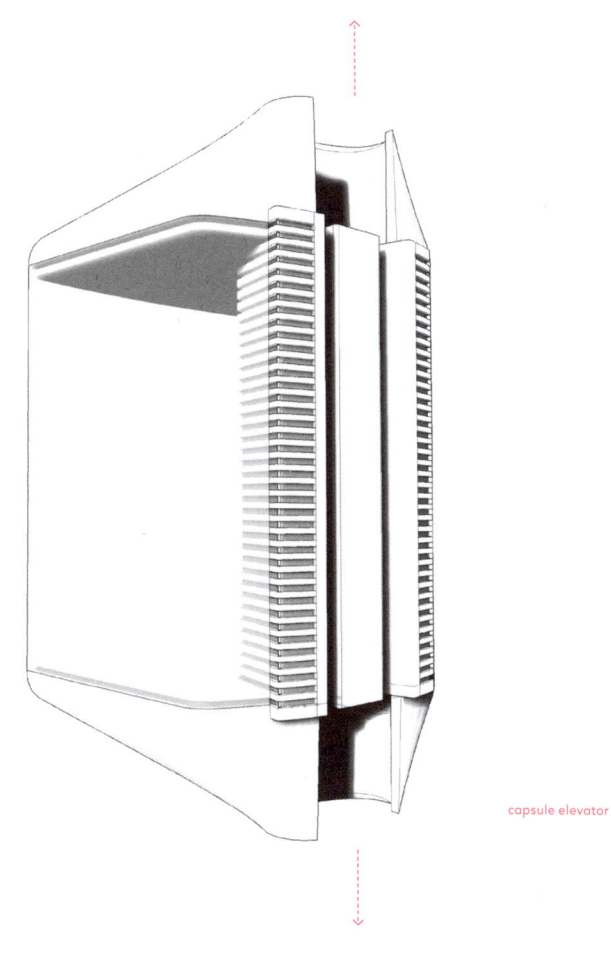

Inhabiting the Topology

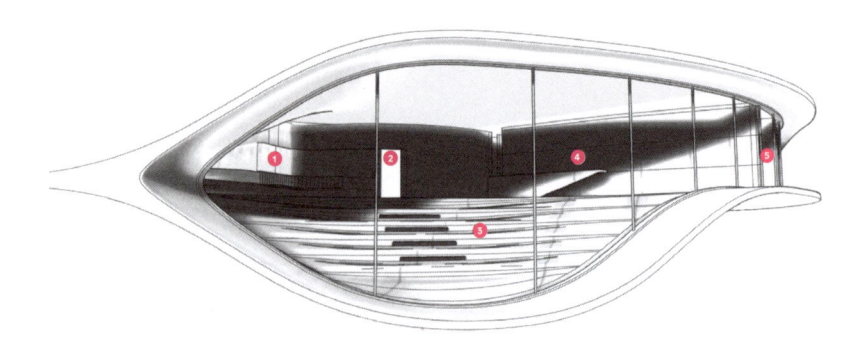

1. living-room
2. entrance
3. garden
4. kitchen
5. bedroom

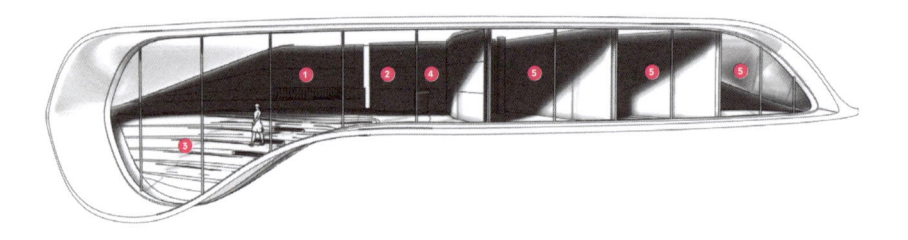

Residential programme

Residential programme

Events & educational programmes

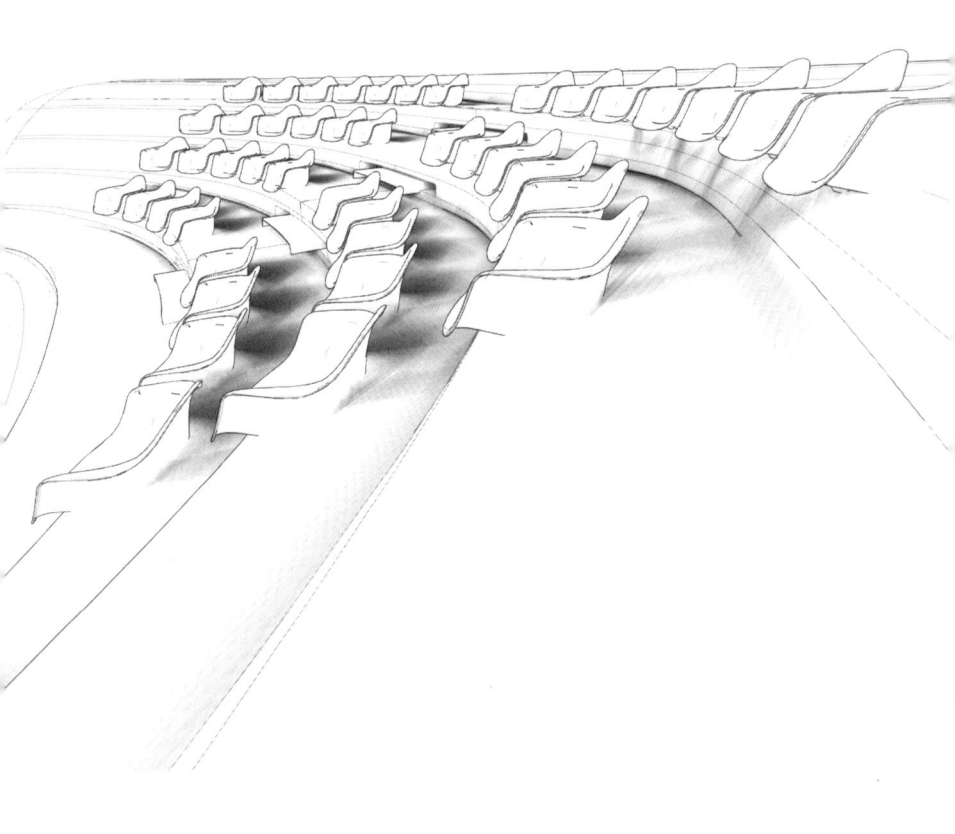

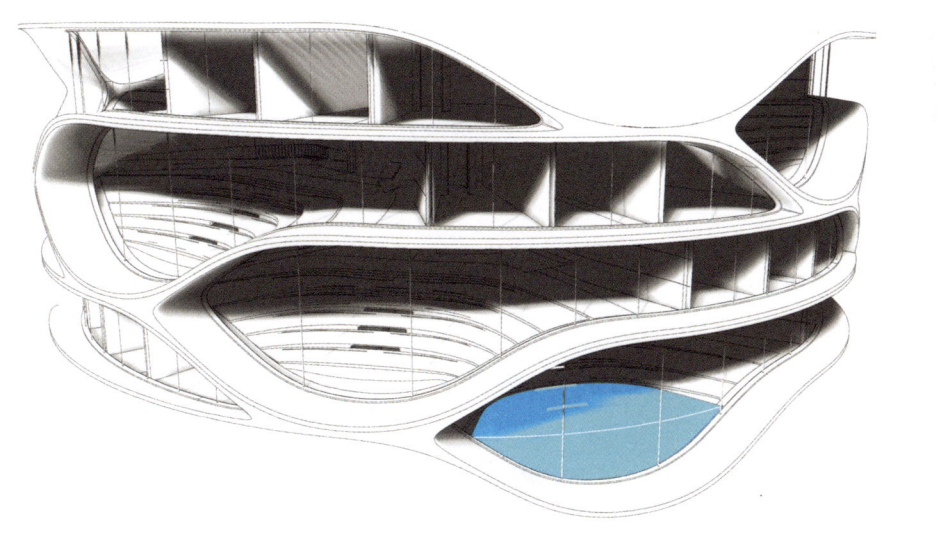

Residential programme - Indoor swimming-pool

Inhabiting the Topology

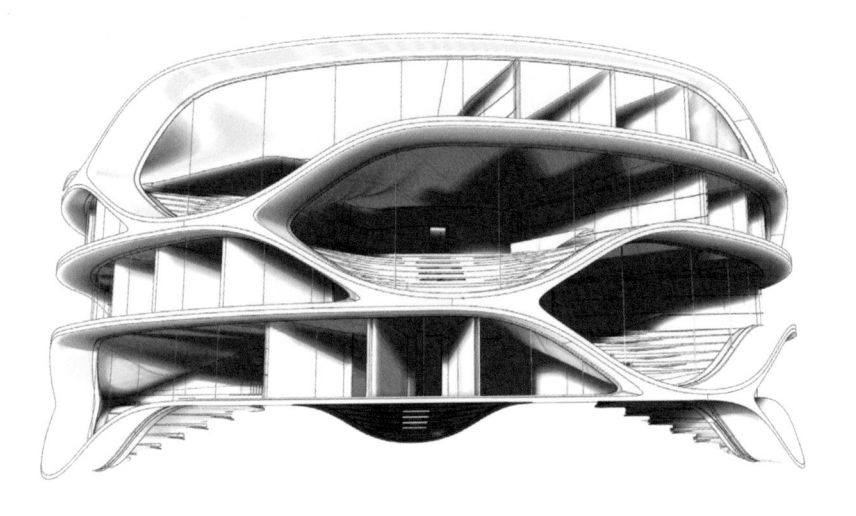

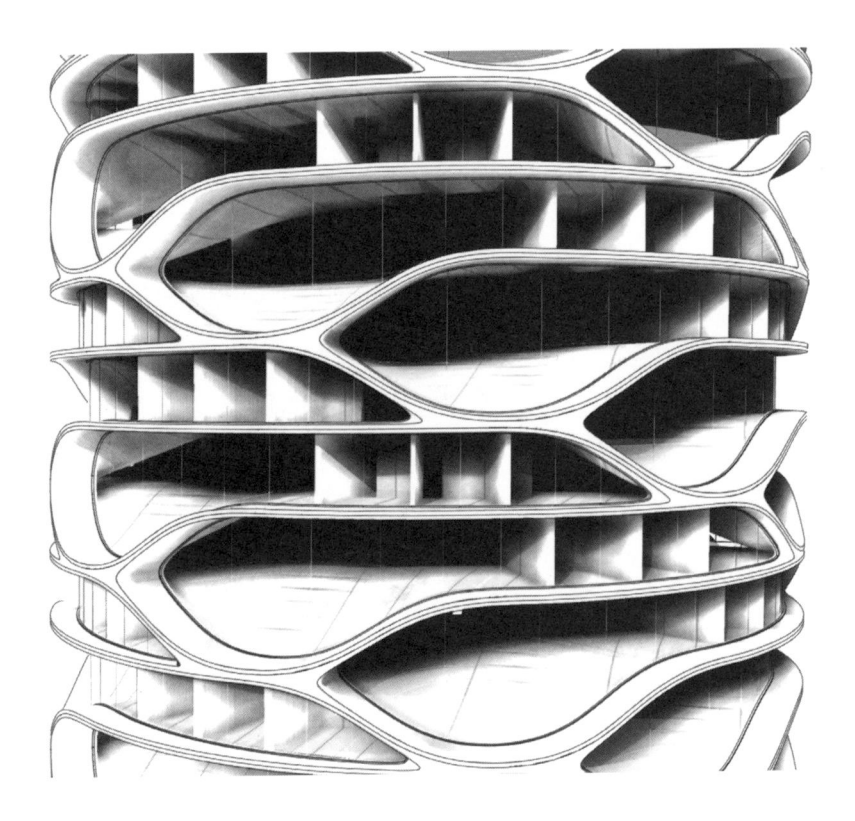

Residential programme

Residential programme

Shadows

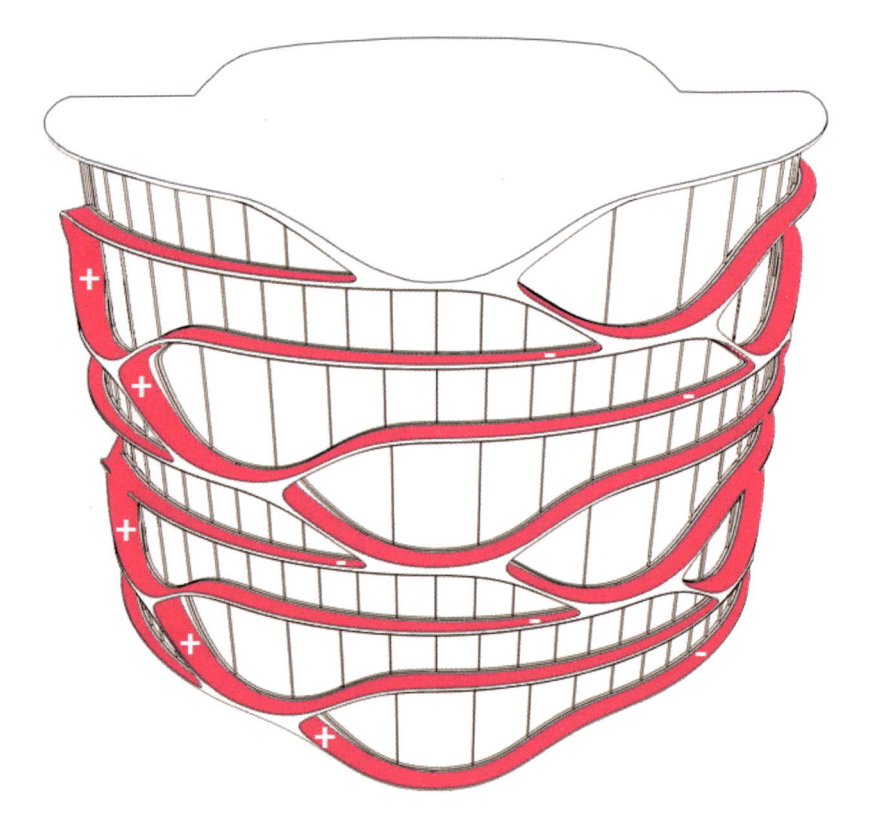

Glazing follows a different curve than the outer concrete, maximizing shadows in the living-rooms

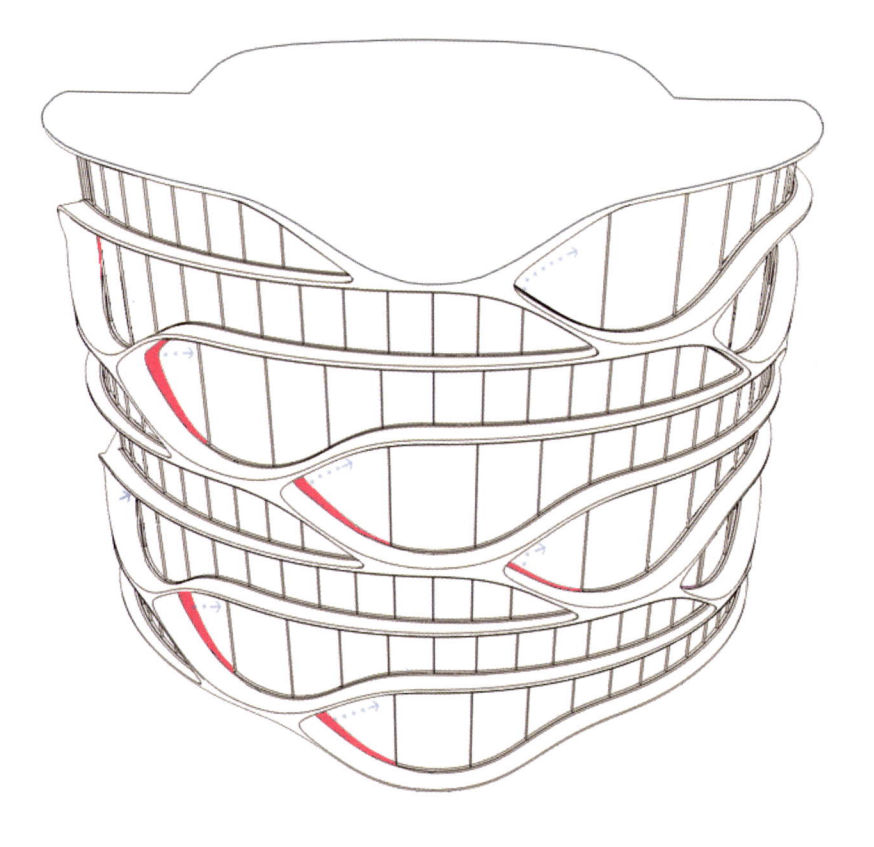

A designed gap between glazing and concrete lets fresh air entering in the units

Vertical Kibbutz

Gran Mediterraneo is at a stage of detailing its programme, its space qualities, and the Mediterranean specificities of its mixed-use activities. The design synthesis of all experiments made on the topology, the technologies involved, the specific location on the Kikar Hamedina, the position of the car-silo, and the Mediterranean green nature, are here developed into schematic plans and three-dimensional sections. The digital techniques of design allow us to visualize precisely how the concrete can be inhabited inside theapartments and the shared public spaces.

Planning to be built using the latest digital technologies, a series of 3d-prints have started as testing prototypes to help the design to progress and to go beyond the pictures that have made Gran Mediterraneo gaining worldwide interest in the international press and the social media, and attract potential clients to adapt it and build it also in other countries.

Using the social typology of a kibbutz as a vehicle for investigation, Gran Mediterraneo takes inspiration into the Israeli version of agricultural co-housing. Parallel to this investigation is a study of urban agriculture which can be applied to the site on both the horizontal and the vertical dimension, exploring the potential of integrating collective living with urban agriculture.

Drawings

1 VEHICLES ACCESS
Access through an inclined ramp to the tower basement.

2 DROP-OFF SERVICE
Instant access to urban life without any detours.

3 CAPSULES
People cross the car-silo in transparent elevators.

4 AUTOMATED CAR-PARK
Car parks itself – efficient parking courtesy of piloted technology.

5 ROBOTS PARK YOUR CAR
Efficient parking in a silo for regular and driverless vehicles.

6 GAINING TIME
More time – less hassle circle.
Piloted parking frees up valuable leisure time.

7 ELECTRIC FUTURE
The car-silo is equipped for electric vehicles.

8 INDUCTIVE CHARGING
Charging the car while parking.

9 CAR ON DEMAND
Providing individualized premium mobility via service app.

10 ACCESS FROM THE PLAZA
Car-free entrance to the tower.

11 MEDITERRANEAN NATURE
Spiral open-air park as buffer space separated from cars.

12 RESIDENTIAL LOBBY
Transfer level from capsules to regular elevators

13 HOTEL GARDEN RESTAURANT
Floor welcoming hotel residents to a bar and a restaurant.

14 ELEVATORS TO THE TOP
Starting from the elevated lobby, 4 elevators stop at each floor of the hotel and of the above kibbutz.

15 HOTEL
The hotel comprises 108 bedrooms on 12 floors.
Every floor welcomes 9 bedrooms of which 3 are suites.

16 VERTICAL FARM
Two floors of shared agriculture separate the hotel from the kibbutz residence.

17 VERTICAL KIBBUTZ
Agriculture oriented co-housings with shared facilities.

18 COLLECTIVE FACILITIES
Kibbutz apartments share a canteen, classrooms and amphitheatres for events.

19 TOWER TECHNICAL FLOOR
The last floor welcomes machines and is surrounded by a vertical farm maintained by the kibbutz residents

20 DEAD SEA SPA CARE
The tower rooftop is an open-air spa dedicated to the dead sea cares.

21 NATURAL POOLS
Every apartment or hotel suite welcomes a natural swimming-pool in the double-height spaces, where water is filtered by aquatic specific plants.

Gran Mediterraneo, 3d section

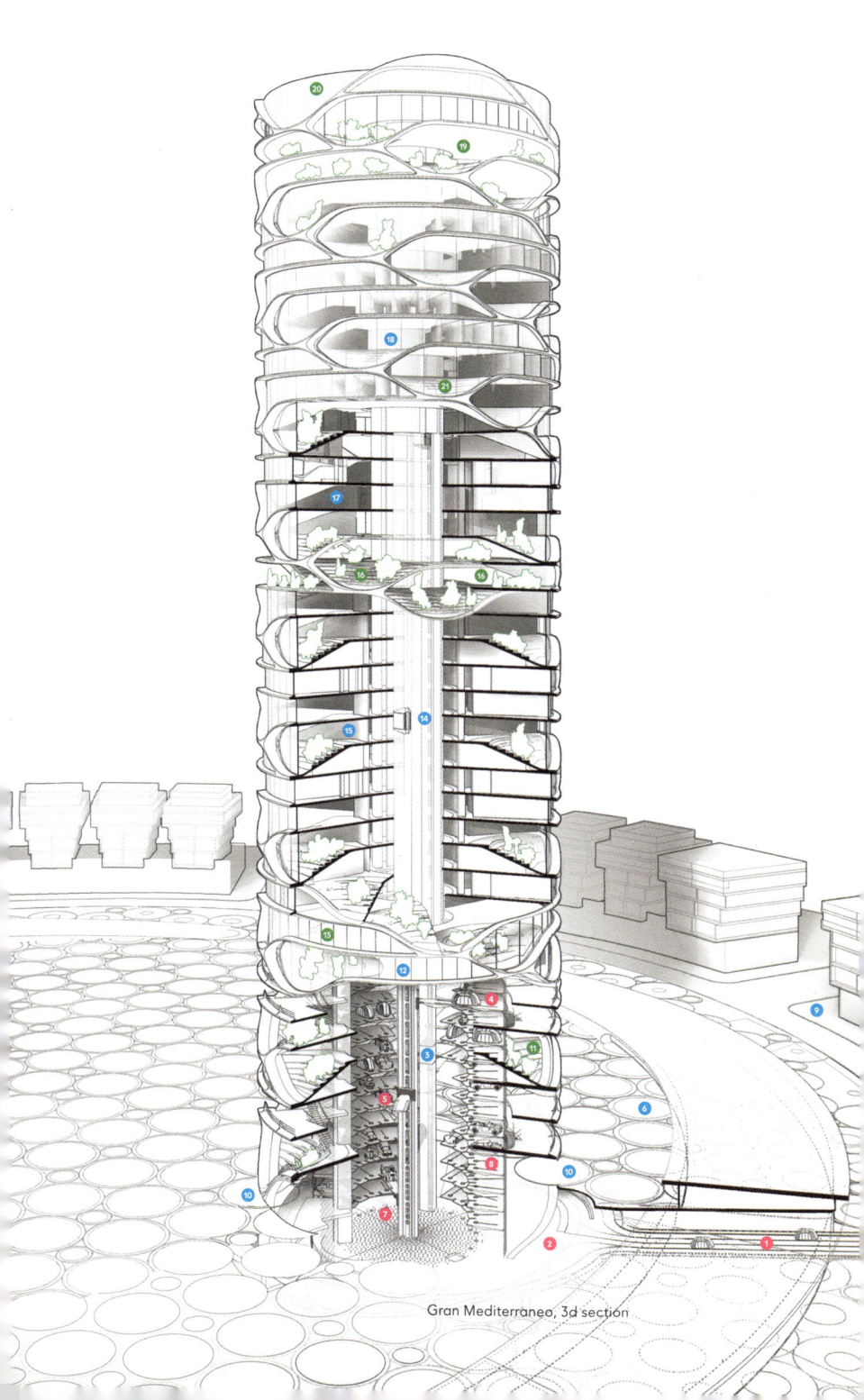

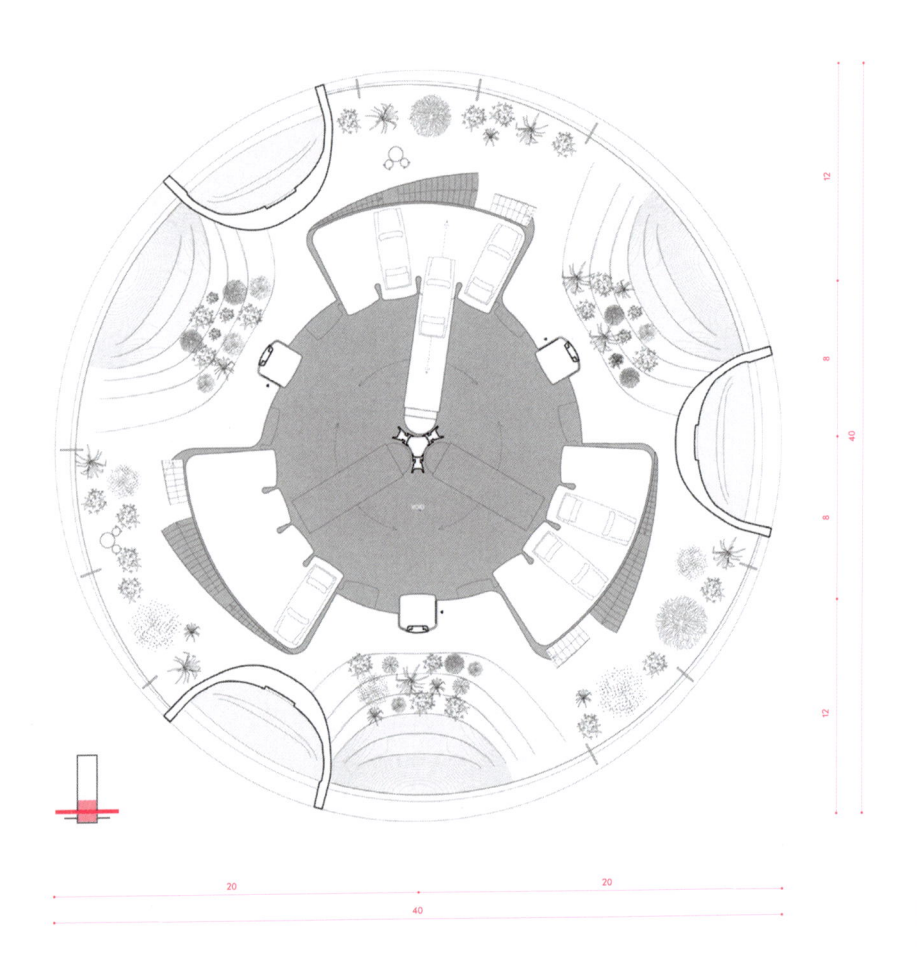

Vertical Kibbutz

Shared car silo and vertical Mediterranean park, typical plan

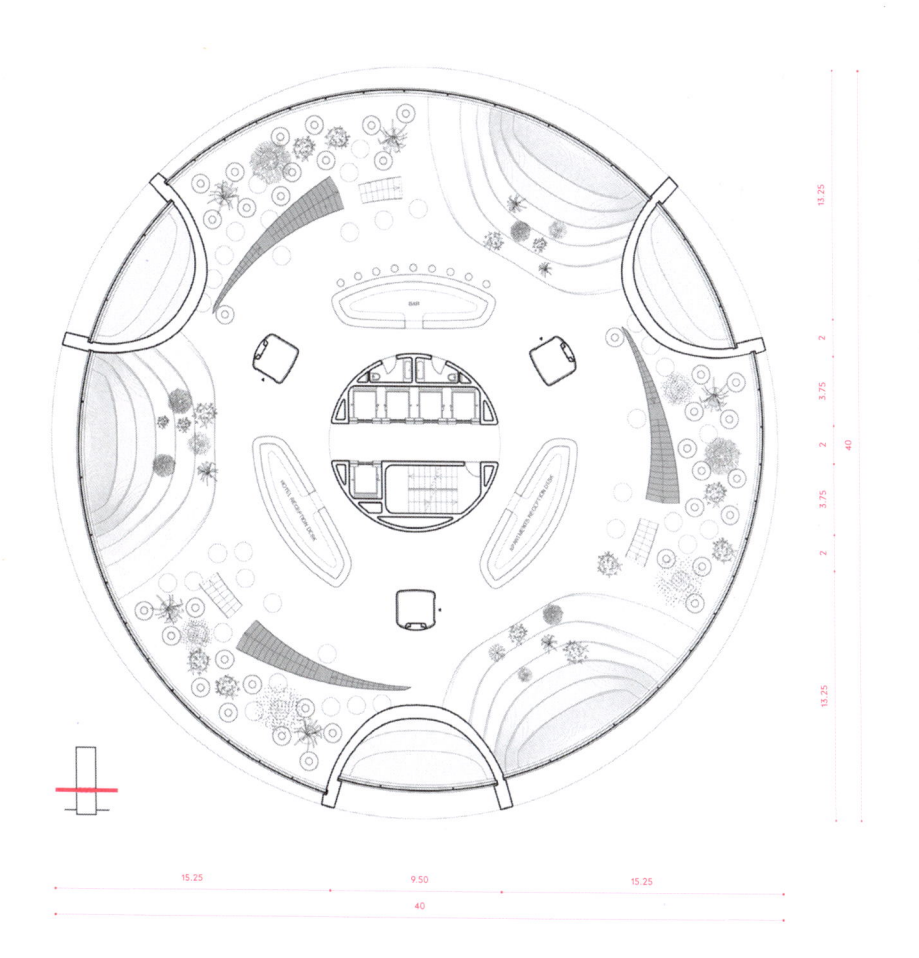

180 Vertical Kibbutz

Elevated residential lobby, plan

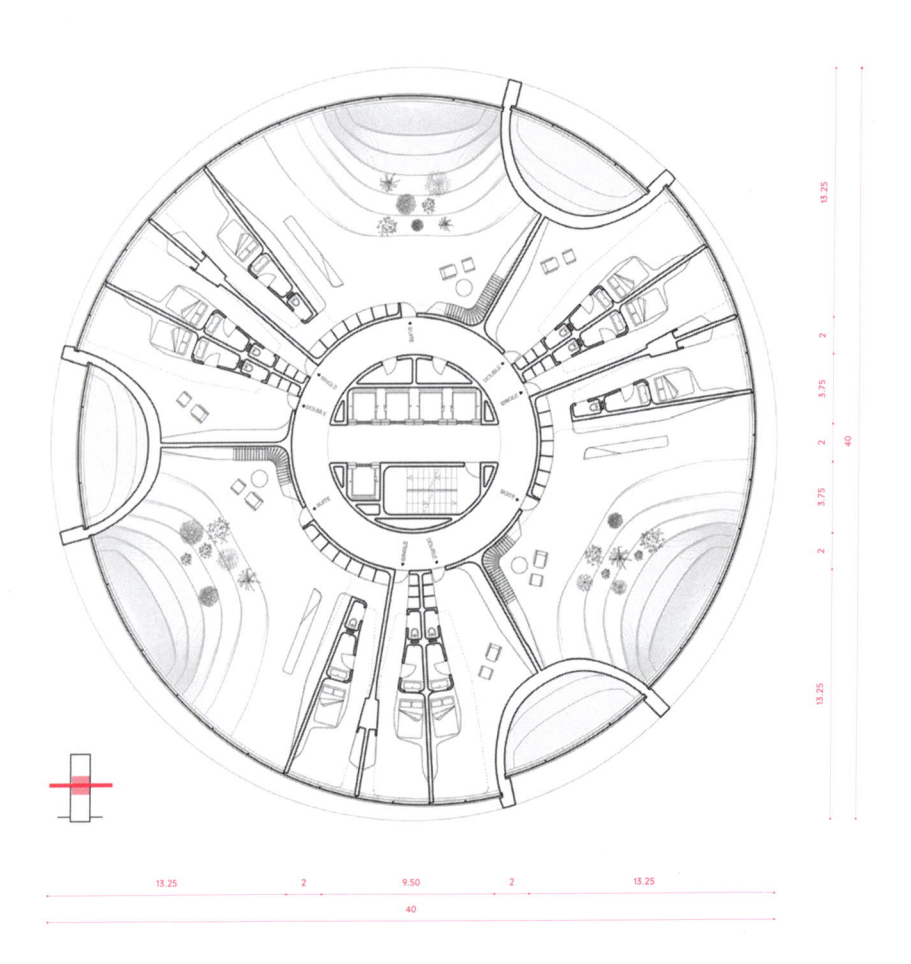

Vertical Kibbutz

Hotel bedrooms, typical plan

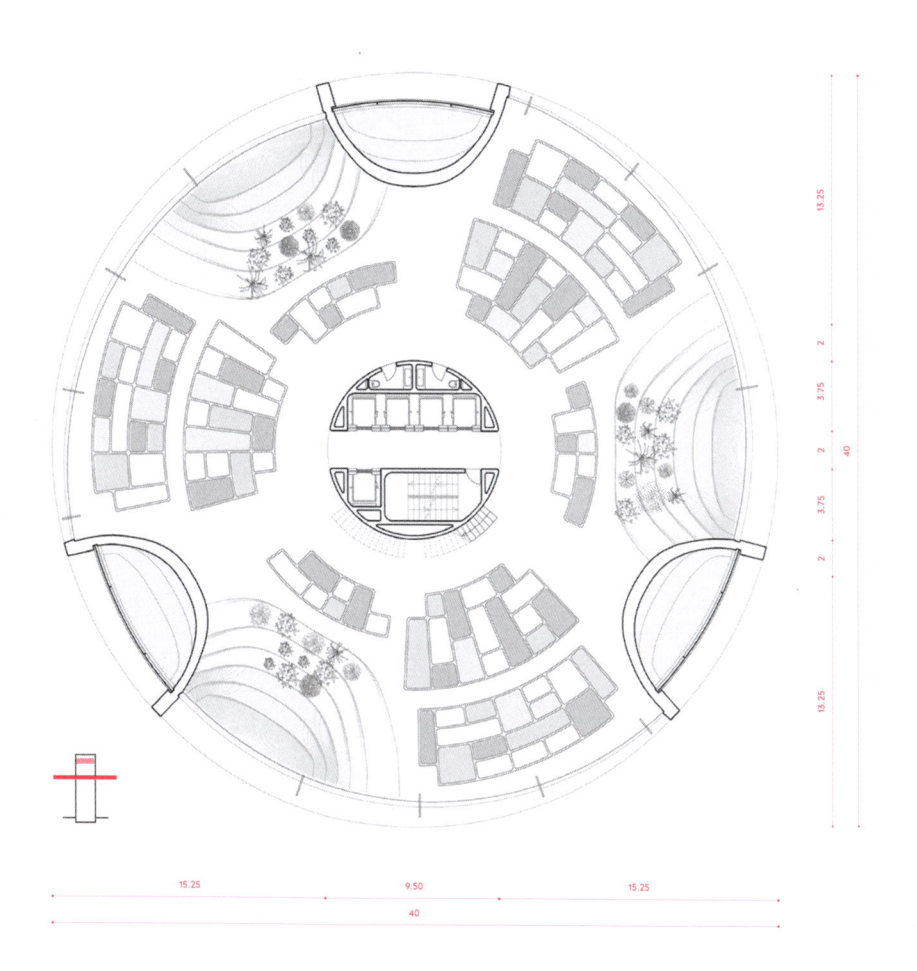

Vertical Kibbutz

Vertical farming and shared agriculture, typical plan

Co-housing and shared activities, typical plan

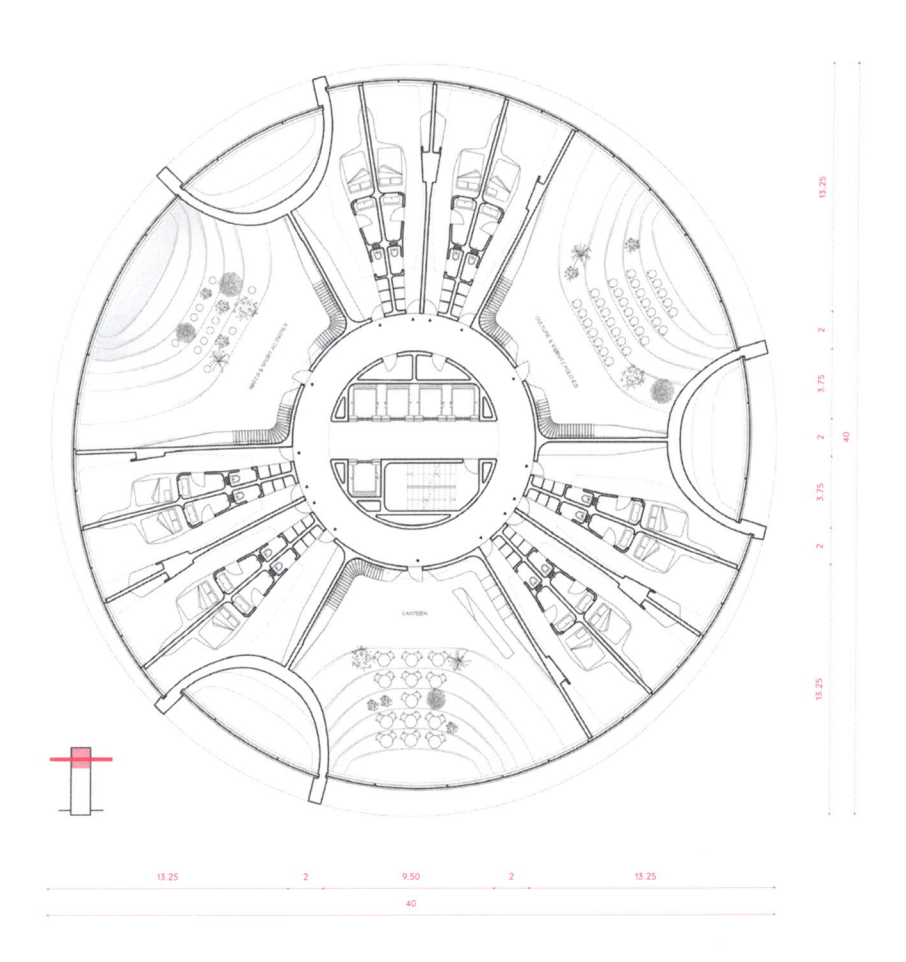

Height: 140 m
Location case study:
Kikar Hamedina, Tel Aviv, Israel
Ground footprint: 1,256 sqm
Total floor area: 54,000 sqm
Main materials: white concrete, clear glass

Level 0 | Kikar Hamedina
Pedestrian access to elevators and to the vertical Mediterranean park, located along the the car silo.

Levels -5 > +8 | Car Silo
14 levels of automated car-parking
Each parking level has 12 parking spaces.
168 parking spaces in total.
Car access by an underground ramp.

Level 9 | Hotel Lobby
Reception desks and concierges.
Transfer floor between parking and residential programmes.
Change of elevators.

Level 10 | Hotel Restaurant and Bar
Public restaurants and bars with panoramic views on the city.

Levels 11 > 22 | Hotel Bedrooms
108 Bedrooms: including singles, doubles and suites.

Levels +22, +23, +36 | Vertical Farms
Shared gardens

Levels +24 > +35 | Apartments
144 Flexible 3-bedroom apartments including flexible and collective spaces for education, coworking and events.

Levels +37, +38 | Spas
Indoor and open-air dead sea spas and pools.

Gran Mediterraneo's Programme

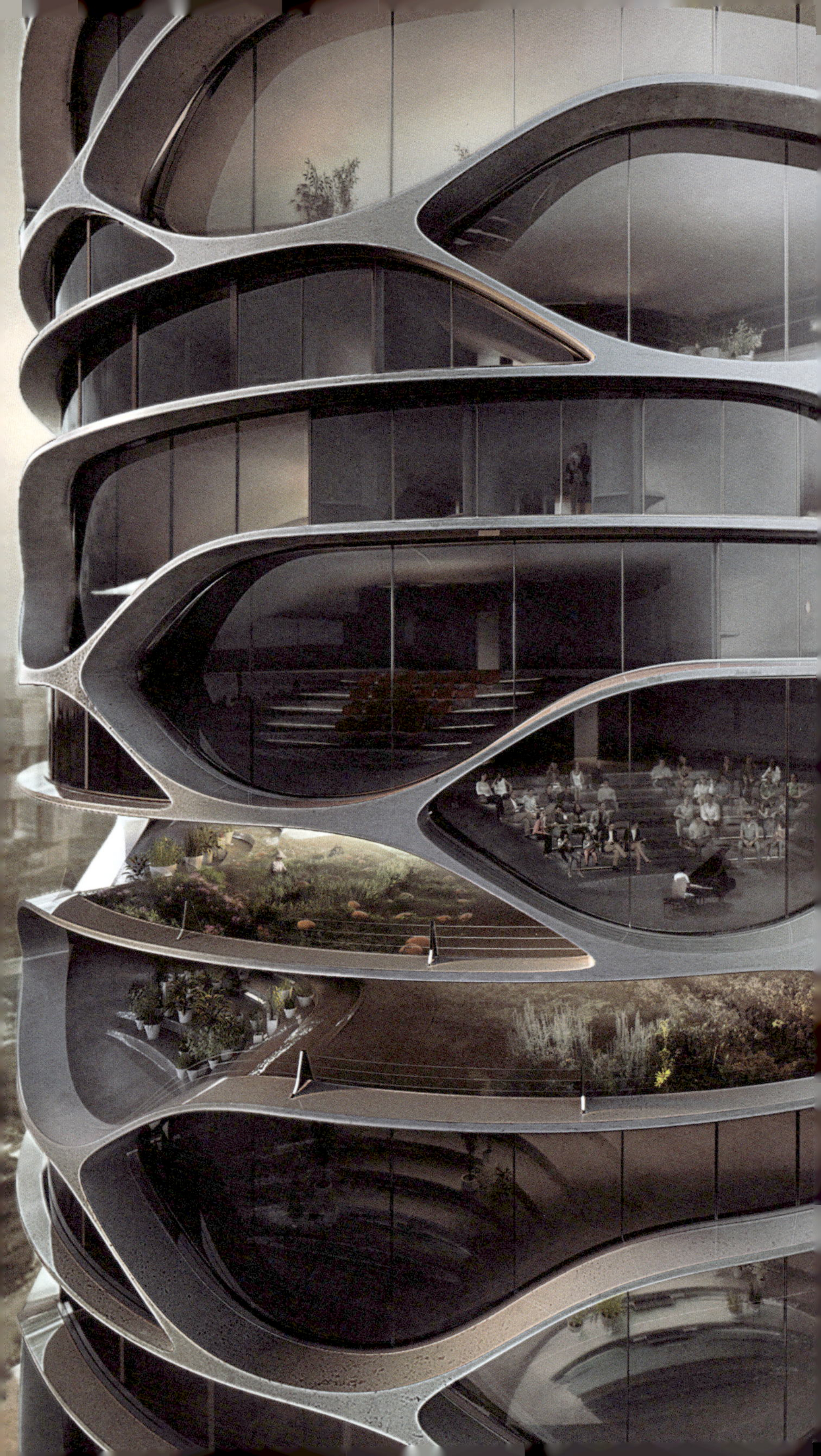

Gran Mediterraneo At Nightfall

187

On Transformed Kikar Hamedina

189

Inside the Automated Car Silo

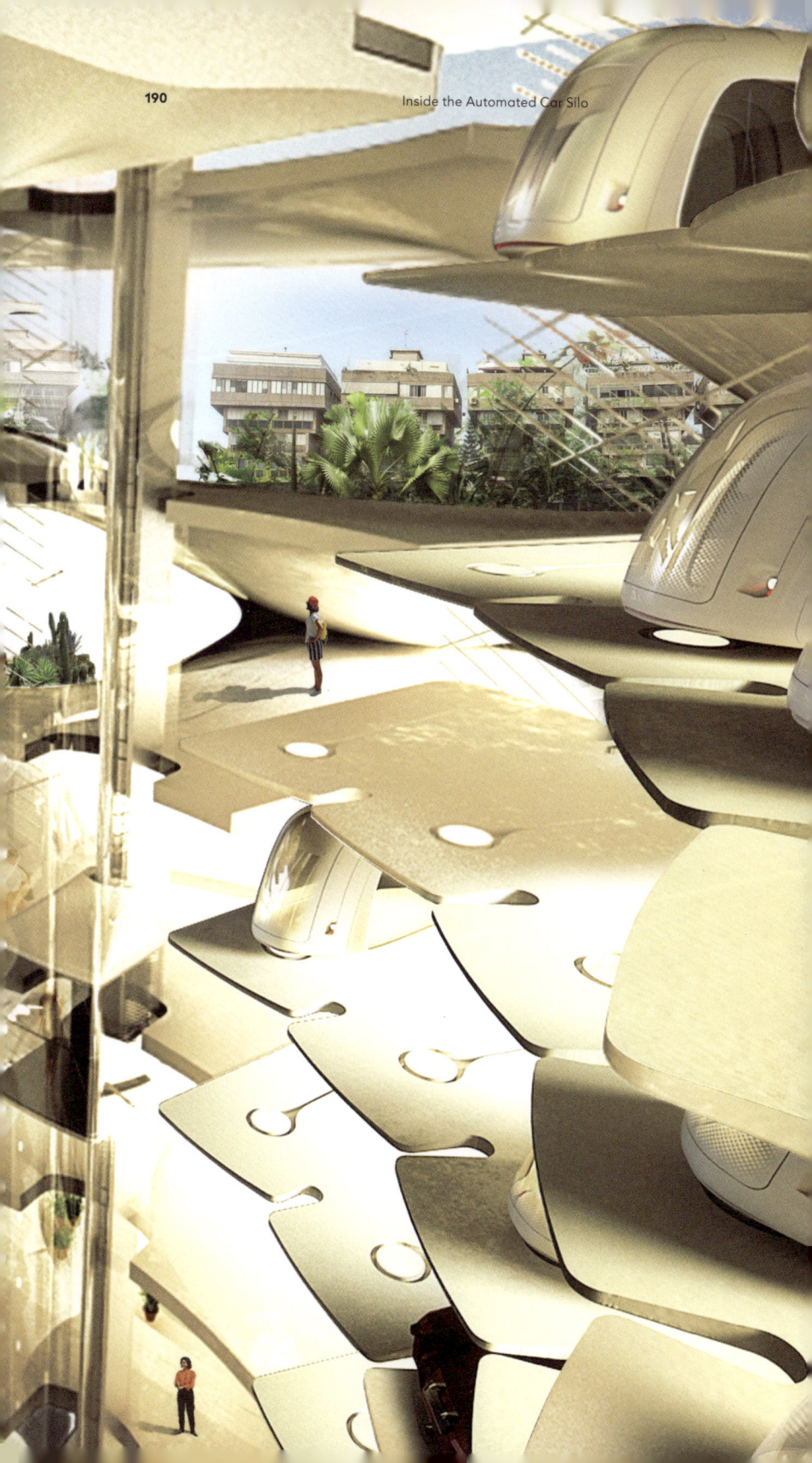

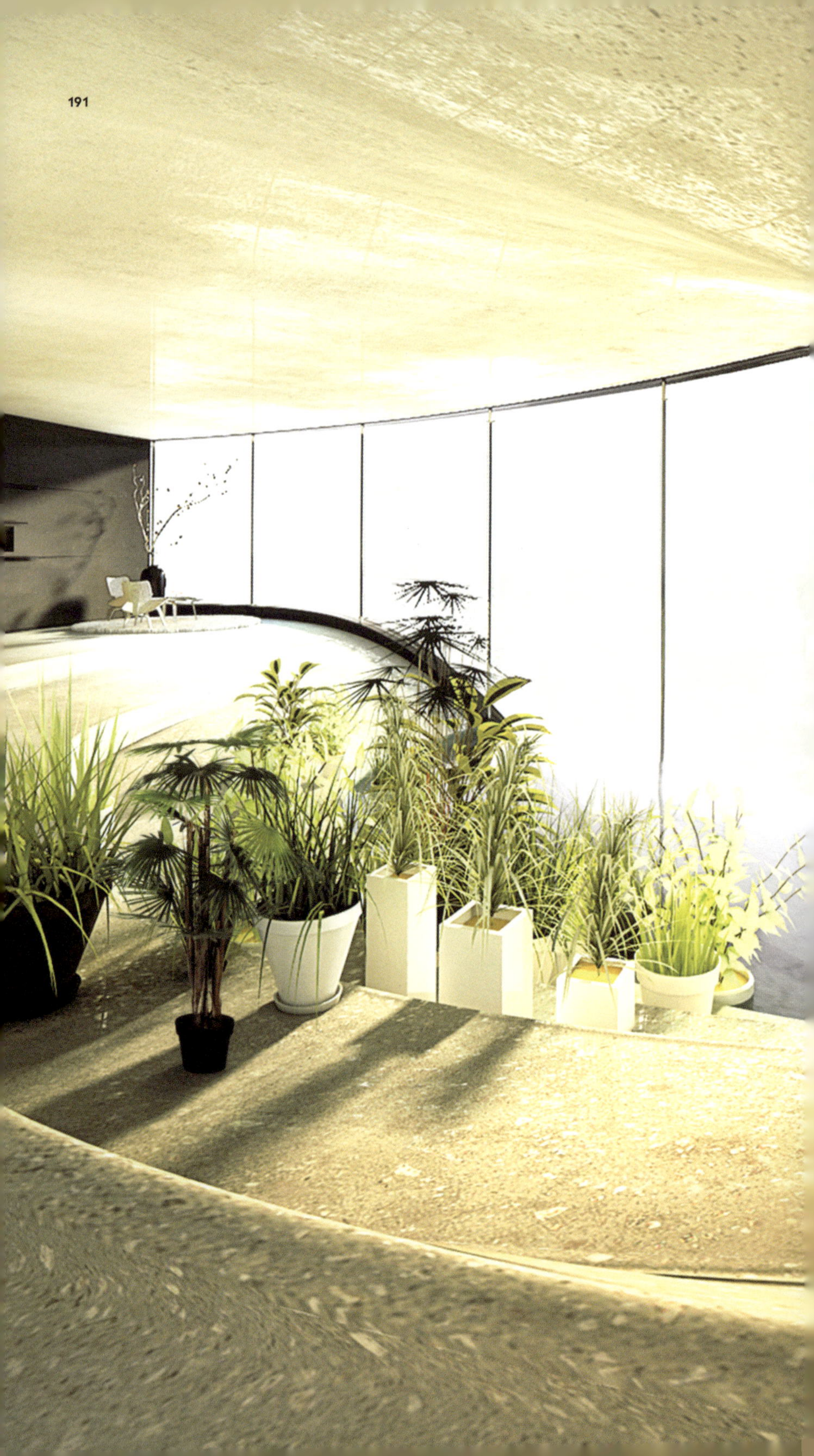

Inside a Residential Unit

193

A Shared Living-Room With View On The White City

195

White Concrete Curves For The White City

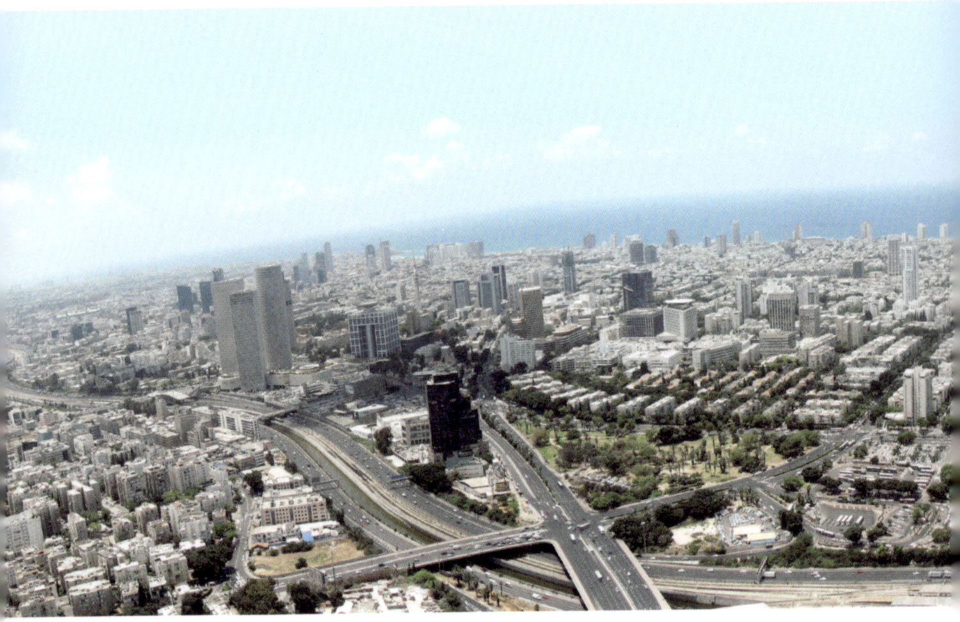

Panoramic view of Tel Aviv

Tel Aviv's panorama with Gran Mediterraneo located on Kikar Hamedina

Building With Technology

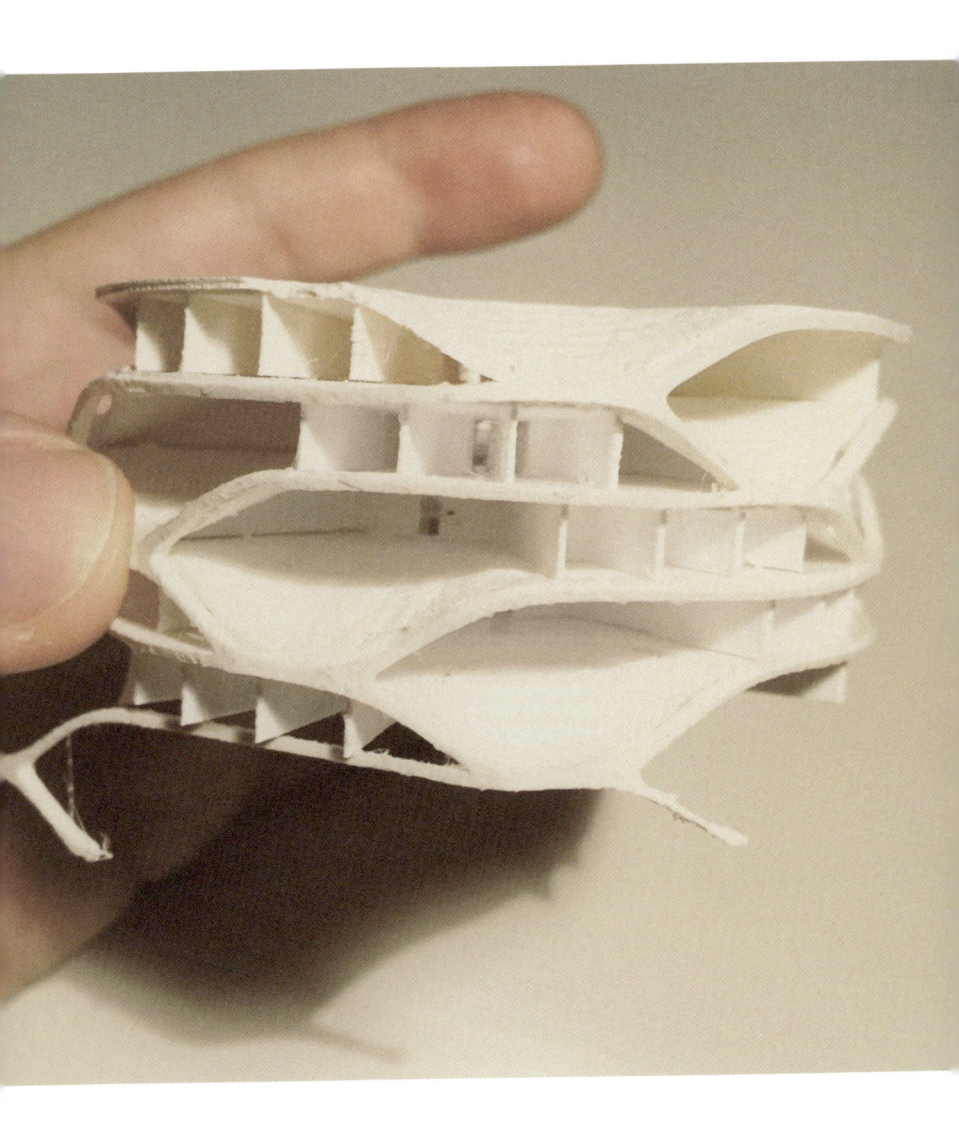

95

3d print test model

Solo exhibition at the AAN+1 Gallery, Paris, France, September 2016 - 3d printed model

Appendix

PROJECT

p.18 fig. 01 Photomontage © Moshe Vrobitzky, 1934, Source 1: Megilat Hahistadrout, Editor M. Bogdan, Tel Aviv; Source 2: Donner, Batia; To Live with the Dream (Exhibition-Catalogue, Tel Aviv Museum of Art), Tel Aviv: Dvir, 1989

p.19 fig. 02 Aerial photograph of Northern Tel Aviv and Dizengoff Circle, circa 1939; Courtesy of the Central Zionist Archives; Photograph © Zultan Kluger

p.20 fig. 03 Braun House, 49 Ahad Ha'am Street / Mazeh Street, 1933, Zaky Chelouche Architect; Photograph © David Tajchman 2017

p.20 fig. 04 Soskin House, 12 Lilienblum Street, 1933, Ze'ev Rechter Architect; Photograph © David Tajchman 2017

p.21 fig. 05 The Ship House (Shimon Levi House), 56 Lavandah Street / Hamasger Street, 1934-1935, Arieh Cohen Architect; Photograph © David Tajchman 2017

p.22 fig. 06 House, 31 Mazeh Street, 1934, M. Rosengarten Architect; Photograph © David Tajchman 2017

p.23 fig. 07 Feldmann House, 18 Bialik Street, 1934, Emanuel & Eliyahu Friedman Architects; Photograph © David Tajchman 2017

p.23 fig. 08 Biegelmann House, 11 Shlomo Hamelekh Street / Tel Hai Street, 1934, Avraham Kabiri Architect; Photograph © David Tajchman 2017

p.24 fig. 09 Reisfeld House, 96 Hayarkon Street, 1935, Pinchas Biezunsky Architect; Photograph © David Tajchman 2017

p.25 fig. 10 Shalem House, 28 Rosh Pina Street, 1935, Arieh Cohen Architect; Photograph © David Tajchman 2017

p.25 fig. 11 Buxenboim House, 6 Bilu Street, 1935, Arieh Streimer Architect; Photograph © David Tajchman 2017

p.26 fig. 12 Bruno House, 3 Strauss Street, 1935, Ze'ev Haller Architect; Photograph © David Tajchman 2017

p.27 fig. 13 Leon Recanati House, 35 Menahem Begin road / 79 Mazeh street, 1935, Salomon Liaskowsky & Jacov Ornstein Architects; Photograph © David Tajchman 2017

p.28 fig. 14 Shaltiel House, 3 Nachalat Binyamin Street, 1935, Arieh Cohen Architect; Photograph © David Tajchman 2017

p.28 fig. 15 Greenberg House, 39 Trumpeldor Street, 1935, Shlomo Erlich Architect; Photograph © David Tajchman 2017

p.29 fig. 16 House Ben-David, 60 Frishman Street, 1936, Aaron Shiffman Architect; Photograph © David Tajchman 2017

p.30 fig. 17 Hornstein House, 48 Dizengoff Street / 54 King George Street, 1936, Ze'ev Haller Architect; Photograph © David Tajchman 2017

p.31 fig. 18 Ya'acov Hanoch House, 10 Aharonovitch Street / Glickson Street, 1937, Richard Barzilai & Shmuel Haussmann Architects; Photograph © David Tajchman 2017

p.32 fig. 19 Esther Cinema (formerly Dizengoff Cinema), Zina Dizengoff Circle / 1 Zamenhof Street, 1939, Yehuda & Raphael Magidovitch Architects; Photograph © David Tajchman 2017

p.37 fig. 20 EL AL Building, 1963, Dov & Ram Karmi & Zvi Meltzer Architects; Photograph © David Tajchman 2017

p.38 fig. 21 Metzudat Zeev (Beit Jabotinsky), 1962-1964, Mordecai Ben Horin Architect; Photograph © Shem Tov Sasson, 2015

p.39 fig. 22 Shalom Meir Tower, Yitzhak Pearlstein, Gideon Ziv & Meir Levy Architects; Photograph © David Tajchman, 2018

p.40 fig. 23 Spiral High-Rise, Zvi Hecker with Alfred Neumann & Eldar Sharon Architects; 1965, Tel Aviv, Unbuilt; Photograph of a study model for a spiral high-rise © Zvi Hecker Architect

p.41 fig. 24 Asia House, 1969-1976, Mordecai Ben Horin Architect; Photograph © David Tajchman 2017

p.42 fig. 25 Dizengoff Residential Tower,

Appendix

1980-1985, Mordecai Ben Horin Architect; Photograph© David Tajchman 2017

p.43 fig. 26 Spiral Apartment House, 1984-1989, Ramat Gan, Israel, Zvi Hecker Architect; Photograph©Michael Krüger Architekturfotografie

p.44 fig. 27 Azrieli Center, 1996-2007, Eli Attia + Moore Yaski Sivan Architects; Photograph © David Tajchman 2017

p.45 fig. 28 Tel Aviv Museum of Art, 2007-2011, Preston Scott-Cohen Architects; Photograph © Hufton + Crown

p.46 fig. 29 Tel Aviv Museum of Art, 2007-2011, Preston Scott-Cohen Architects; Photograph © Hufton + Crown

p.47 fig. 30 "Deportation" © Victor Enrich 2011

p.48 fig. 31 Rothschild Tower, 2007-2017, Richard Meier & Partners Architects LLP; Rendering ©Richard Meier & Partners Architects LLP

p.51 fig. 32 Aerial view of Moshav Nahalal from southeast to northwest, Richard Kauffmann Architect; Date of picture (year): 1938, Photograph © Hans Kashuv, identified and dated by Prof. Yossi Ben-Artzi (Department of Land of Israel Studies, University of Haifa), Collection: The corporal album - Younes and Soraya Nazarian Library at the University of Haifa Younes and Soraya Nazarian Library - University of Haifa

p.52 fig. 33 Workers in the field, training period of the new immigrants at Kibbutz Na'an; Date of picture (year): 1935, Photograph credits: Courtesy of Hagai Ben-Gurion, 2006, Courtesy of Nadav Man, Bitmuna, Collection: Arie Ben-Gurion Younes and Soraya Nazarian Library - University of Haifa

p.53 fig. 34 Members of the Mahanot Haolim loading hay at Kibbutz Na'an; Date of picture (year): 1935, Photograph credits: Courtesy of Hagai Ben-Gurion, 2006, Courtesy of Nadav Man, Bitmuna, Collection: Arie Ben-Gurion Younes and Soraya Nazarian Library - University of Haifa

p.54 fig. 35 A student taking care of chickens at Moshav Nahalal; Date of picture (year): 1940-48, Photographer: Moshe Schwartz, Photograph credits: Courtesy of Trudy Schwartz-Aliar, 2006, Courtesy of Nadav Man, Bitmuna, Collection: Schwartz Younes and Soraya Nazarian Library - University of Haifa

p.54 fig. 36 Ziva Heifetz (on the right) and her friend Ella at Moshav Nahalal; Date of picture (year): 1936, Photographer: Moshe Schwartz, Photograph credits: Courtesy of Family Heifetz, 2006, Courtesy of Nadav Man, Bitmuna, Collection: Schwartz Younes and Soraya Nazarian Library - University of Haifa

p.54 fig. 37 Potted plants in the nursery at Moshav Nahalal; Date of picture (year): 1940-48, Photographer: Moshe Schwartz, Photograph credits: Courtesy of Trudy Schwartz Aliar, 2006, Courtesy of Nadav Man, Bitmuna, Collection: Schwartz Younes and Soraya Nazarian Library - University of Haifa

p.55 fig. 38 First girls born in Kibbutz Bet Hashitta; Date of picture (year): 1936, Photograph credits: Courtesy of Nurit Moran Sarig, 2007, Courtesy of Nadav Man, Bitmuna Younes and Soraya Nazarian Library - University of Haifa

p.55 fig. 39 Children near an artificial lake, Kibbutz Merhavya; Date of picture (year): 1940-48,Photographer: Moshe Schwartz, Photograph credits: Courtesy of Trudy Schwartz-Aliar, 2006, Courtesy of Nadav Man, Bitmuna, Collection: Schwartz Younes and Soraya Nazarian Library - University of Haifa

p.55 fig. 40 Children at Kibbutz En Harod; Photograph credits: Courtesy of Assaf David Afer, Courtesy of Nadav Man, Bitmuna, Younes and Soraya Nazarian Library - University of Haifa

p.56 fig. 41 Girls celebrating the first fruits, Kibbutz Merhavya; Date

Appendix

of picture (year): 1930-1950, Photographer: Naftali Oppenheim, Photograph credits: Courtesy of Jordan Valley Regional Council Archives, Courtesy of Nadav Man, Bitmuna, Collection: Schwartz Younes and Soraya Nazarian Library - University of Haifa

p.56 fig. 42 Seder Pesach at Kibbutz Merhavya; Date of picture (year): 1940-48, Photographer: Moshe Schwartz, Photograph credits: Courtesy of Trudy Schwartz-Aliar, 2006, Courtesy of Nadav Man, Bitmuna, Collection: Schwartz Younes and Soraya Nazarian Library - University of Haifa

p.57 fig. 43 Summer camp children valley; Date of picture (year): 1941, Photograph credits: Courtesy of Hagai Ben-Gurion, 2006, Courtesy of Nadav Man, Bitmuna Collection: Arie Ben-Gurion Younes and Soraya Nazarian Library - University of Haifa

p.57 fig. 44 Volleyball players; Date of picture (year): 1941, Photograph credits: Courtesy of Hagai Ben-Gurion, 2006, Courtesy of Nadav Man, Bitmuna Collection: Arie Ben-Gurion Younes and Soraya Nazarian Library - University of Haifa

p.57 fig. 45 The first camp headquarters of the kibbutz members at Kibbutz Giv'at Brener; Date of picture (year): 1952, Photograph credits: Courtesy of Hagai Ben-Gurion, 2006, Courtesy of Nadav Man, Bitmuna, Collection: Arie Ben-Gurion Younes and Soraya Nazarian Library - University of Haifa

p.58 fig. 46 Music class in Ramat Hadassah Szold; Date of picture (year): 1958, Photograph credits: Courtesy of the Hadassah Medical Center Ein Kerem in Jerusalem, 2006, Courtesy of Nadav Man, Bitmuna, Collection: Arie Ben-Gurion Younes and Soraya Nazarian Library - University of Haifa

p.58 fig. 47 Painter working at Kibbutz Merhavya; Date of picture (year): 1940-48, Photographer: Moshe Schwartz, Photograph credits: Courtesy of Trudy Schwartz-Aliar, 2006, Courtesy of Nadav Man, Bitmuna, Collection: Schwartz Younes and Soraya Nazarian Library - University of Haifa

p.60 fig. 48 Golf cart at Kibbutz Sha'ar Ha'Amakim, 2016; Illustration David Tajchman 2017

p.61 fig. 49 Collective Intercity Taxi, Israel; Illustration David Tajchman 2017

p.62 fig. 50 Ayalon highway, Tel Aviv; Photograph © David Tajchman 2017

p.63 fig. 51 Works on Menahem Begin Boulevard; Photograph © David Tajchman 2017

p.65 fig. 52 Buckminster "Bucky" Fuller - Fly's Eye Dome and Dymaxion Car; Photograph © Roger White Stoller, 1980, black and white

p.66 fig. 53 Citroën DS 19 Cabriolet, press presentation 1961; courtesy of © L'Aventure Peugeot Citroën DS - Tous droits réservés

p.67 fig. 54 Electricity May Be The Driver; Image Courtesy of © the Advertising Archives

p.68 fig. 55 Firebird III, General Motors, Motorama; Photograph © GM

p.69 fig. 56 Better Place, Electric Battery Switching Station, 2008-2014, Israel; Photograph © Better Place

p.69 fig. 57 Autolib', Electric, Cecomp, Pininfarina Design, Paris; Photograph courtesy © Autolib'

p.70 fig. 58 Driverless Personal Rapid Transit (PRT) System, Electric, Masdar City; Photograph courtesy © Masdar

p.70 fig. 59 Waymo Self-Driving Vehicle (previously Google Car), California, USA; Photograph © Waymo

p.71 fig. 60 Mercedes-Benz F015; Photograph by Tobias C. Hutzler © Daimler AG; Set Design "IAA Folder" by Sarah Illenberger in collaboration with Tammo Prinz for Antoni/ Berlin, 2015

p.77 fig. 61 Fiat Factory, Pista del Lingotto, Giacomo Mattè Trucco Architect Engineer, Turin, Italy; Photograph © Centro e Archivio Storico Fiat

p.78 fig. 62 Marina City, Bertrand

Goldberg Architect, Chicago, USA, Courtesy of Geoffrey Goldberg; Photograph © Amandine Isoardi & Julien Vietto

p.79 fig. 63 Autostadt, Volkswagen Car Park, Henn Architekten, Wolfsburg, Germany; Photograph © Lars Landmann / Autostadt

p.80 fig. 64 Mercedez-Benz Museum, UNStudio, Stuttgart, Germany, 2001-2006; Photograph © Brigida Gonzalez

p.81 fig. 65 1111 Lincoln Road, Herzog & De Meuron Architects, Miami, USA; Photograph © Hufton + Crow

p.85 fig. 66 Hatra, Iraq, source 1: General plan of Hatra based on Aggoula, B., Inventaire des inscriptions hatréennes, (Paris, 1991), XXVII, source 2: Jabar Khalil Ibrahim, Pre-Islamic Settlement in Jazirah, Baghdad, 1986

p.86 fig. 67 Ideal City Layouts, source: 'Etliche Underricht, zu Befestigung der Stett, Schlosz, und Flecken' (1527), Albrecht Dürer, Nürnberg, Germany; Ideal cities from the Renaissance with the emphasis on defense (city walls). 1. La Sforzinda by Filarete (1460 – 1465); 2. Fra Giocondo (Giovanni of Verona), c. 1433 – 1515; 3. Girolamo Magi (or Maggi) (c. 1523 – c. 1572) (1564); 4. Giorgio Vasari (1598); 5. Antonio Lupicini (c. 1530 – c. 1598); 6. Daniele Barbaro (1513 – 1570); 7. Pietro Cattaneo (1537 – 1587); 8/9; Francesco di Giorgio Martini (1439 – 1502).

p.87 fig. 68 Palmanova, Italy; Imagery © 2017 Google, Map Data © 2017 Google

p.88 fig. 69 Karlsruhe, Germany © Karlsruher Stadtansicht, Kupferstich von Heinrich Schwarz, 1721

p.89 fig. 70 Tainan, Taïwan, Map of Tainan with fortifications during Qing Dynasty, source: 1807; unknown author

p.90 fig. 71 Garden City, Diagram No.7, Ebenezer Howard, To-morrow: A Peaceful Path to Real Reform, 1898 Edition, Swan Sonnenschein & Co, United Kingdom

p.91 fig. 72 Moshav Nahalal, Israel, Richard Kauffmann Architect 1921; Photograph© Zeev Stein, 2016; Creative Commons Attribution-ShareAlike 4.0 International CC BY-SA 4.0

p.92 fig. 73 Particle Accelerator Complex, CERN - European Organization for Nuclear Research, Franco-Swiss Border, Aerial view of the CERN; Photo by © Maximilien Brice (CERN), 2008

p.93 fig. 74 Aéroport Charles De Gaulle Terminal 1, 1967-1974, Paul Andreu Architect, Roissy, France; Photograph ©David Tajchman 2017

p.94 fig. 75 Airport Cities; source 1: Conway H. M. (1993): Airport Cities 21: The New Global Transport Centers of the 21st Century, © Conway Data, Inc., source 2: 20th Century Concepts for 21st Century Airports, 2013, aeroscape.org by Daniel Kraffczyk

PROCESS

p.99 fig. 76 Casa das Canoas, Oscar Niemeyer Architect, Barra da Tijuca, Rio de Janeiro, Brazil; Photograph©Matheus Seco 2017

p.100 fig. 77 Garden and House, Ryue Nishizawa Architect, Tokyo, Japan; Photograph © Gabrielle Toledano 2017

p.103 fig. 78 Hanging gardens of Babylon, 1983, Parque Jaime Duque, Tocancipa, Colombia; Photograph©Nayer Youakim

p.116 fig. 79 Housing buildings: Abba Elhanani Architect Hamedina Circle: Abba Elhanani, Yisrael Lotan & Oscar Niemeyer Architects; Photograph © Evgeniy Everboukh - TLVspot.com

p.118 fig. 80 Unità Residenziale Ovest Olivetti, Ivrea, Italy, 1968-71, Roberto Gabetti and Aimaro Isola Architects, with Luciano Re; Drawing courtesy of © the Archivio Gabetti e Isola, Torino

p.119 fig. 81 Fuji Kindergarten, Tezuka Architects, Tokyo, Japan; Photograph courtesy of © Tezuka Architects

p.123 fig. 82 Man-made ground circular patterns in Teguidda-n-Tessoumt; Images © 2017 Digital Globe © 2017 Google Maps

Appendix

p.124 fig. 83 Double cover of hexagonal packing over two marked circles © Danny Calegari, "Circle packing – theory and practice", Geometry and the Imagination, 2012

p.135 fig. 84 Möbius Strip, 1858; Illustration © David Tajchman

p.136 fig. 85 Klein bottle, 1882; Illustration © David Tajchman

p.137 fig. 86 Natural Hills; Preparatory Sketches, 1955, Heinz Isler © gta archives / ETH Zurich (holding Heinz Isler)

p.138 fig. 87 Restaurant Los Manantiales, Félix Candela Outeriño Architect, Xochimilco, Mexico, Courtesy of © Avery Architectural & Fine Arts Library, Columbia University

p.139 fig. 88 Frederick Kiesler, Model for an "Endless House", New York, 1959, Silvergelatine vintage print on baryta paper; Photograph by George Barrows © 2017 Austrian Frederick and Lillian Kiesler Private Foundation, Vienna

p.140 fig. 89 Tour Sans Fins, Jean Nouvel & Associés, Paris, France, Winning competition 1989, Unbuilt; Illustration © Vincent Lafont

p.141 fig. 90 Möbius House, UNStudio, 't Gooi, the Netherlands, 1993-1998, Built; Photograph © Christian Richters

p.142 fig. 91 'Meiso no Mori' Municipal Funeral Hall, Toyo Ito & Associates, Architects, Kakamigahara, Gifu, Japan, Photograph courtesy of © Toyo Ito & Associates, Architects

p.143 fig. 92 National Taichung Theater, Taïwan, Toyo Ito & Associates, Architects, Physical Model; Photograph courtesy of © Toyo Ito & Associates, Architects

p.144 fig. 93 Villa Ypsilon, Lassa Architects, Finikounda, Greece; Photograph © Lassa © Naaro

p.144 fig. 94 Prototype Droneport Shell, The Norman Foster Foundation with Future Africa, EPFL and, Ochsendorf, DeJong & Block with Block Research Group, ETH Zurich, 2016, Venice, Italy; Photograph © Nigel Young and The Norman Foster Foundation

p.147 — 154 Sketches © David Tajchman
p.155 — 156 Study model © David Tajchman

PROGRESS

p.199 fig. 95 3d Printed model, Luc Izri; Photograph © David Tajchman 2017

p.200 fig. 96 3d printed model, 2016, scale 1/500°: Luc Izri, David Tajchman, Solo Exhibition at the Gallery AAN+1, Paris, France, September 201; Photograph © Maria Smigielska

Acknowledgements

The production of this book has relied on the engagement, the trust and the enthusiasm of precious people.

First and foremost, our deep thanks go to Luc Izri who has considerably contributed to the digital modelling and the architectural design of the projects at the office since 2010, and has produced the first printed model of the Gran Mediterraneo. This book has benefited greatly from his laborious researches by computational design. Together with David Tajchman, they have developed a strong design complicity, which generated very interesting conversations on the work and our design approach at the studio.

We are also thankful to Leslie Ware and Pierre Cutellic, who first believed in the project by inviting David Tajchman to exhibit the Gran Mediterraneo at their Parisian architecture gallery. This solo show was the initial context to produce this book and to start thinking about its written contents: "Project, Process, Progress".

We also greatly appreciate the contribution of Carl Fredrik Svenstedt: his thoughtful introductory essay offers the book a critical foreword with an outside look at our proposal and its aesthetics.

We particularly want to acknowledge the creative, genuine and responsive work of graphic designer Sara Jassim, for her ideas on the layout and the graphic design of this book. Which echoes so precisely the project's identity, its Gesamtkunstwerk spirit and David Tajchman's background in Brussels, the city of Art Nouveau and its main figure: architect Victor Horta.

And last but not least: Narcissa Balta who proofread this book written in English, and brought her views on David Tajchman's writings from another perspective.

This book has been generously supported by Jenny and Yves Tajchman, Barbara Tajchman, Jeremy Bacon, Wayne Ko, Michel Jurowicz and numerous individuals.

Publishers	Actar Publishers
	440 Park Av. South, 17th Floor, New York, NY 10016, USA
Author	Written and edited by David Tajchman
	First edition 2018
Graphic Design	Sara Jassim
Design Team	David Tajchman, Luc Izri
	Gran Mediterraneo is a self-Initiated architectural proposal
	Creative authorship © Architectures David Tajchman 2016
Essays	"Too Beautiful" by Carl Fredrik Svenstedt
	"Future Collectivism" by David Tajchman
Physical Models	Topological study models, 2016, scale 1/200°: David Tajchman
	3d printed model, 2016, scale 1/500°: Luc Izri, David Tajchman
Proofreading	Narcissa Balta
Printing	Comgrafic, Barcelona, Spain
Distribution	Actar D, Inc.
	New York 355 Lexington Avenue, 8th Floor,
	New York, NY 10017, USA
	+ 1 2129662207, salesnewyork@actar-d.com
	Barcelona Roca i Batlle 2-408023 Barcelona, SP
	+ 34 933 282 183, eurosales@actar-d.com
ISBN	978-1-9487650-1-5
PCN number	2018935309
	A CIP catalogue record for this book is available from Library of Congress, Washington, D.C., USA

All rights reserved. No part of this publication may be reproduced, stored in a retrieval system or transmitted in any form or by means of electronic, mechanical, photocopying, recording or otherwise, without the permission of Actar Publishers.

Every effort has been made to gain permission from copyright holders and/or photographers, where known, for the images reproduced in this book, and care has been taken to caption and credit those images correctly. Any omissions are unintentional and we will be happy to make appropriate corrections in future editions if further information is brought to the author's attention.

ACTAR

ARCHITECTURES
DAVID
TAJCHMAN

SARAJASSIM